PROPHETIC DECLARATION
FROM PSALM 23

The Lord is my Shepherd—
I follow His voice alone.

In Him, I lack nothing. He causes me to rest in divine provision and leads me by waters of peace.

He restores my soul and aligns me with righteousness–for the honor of His holy name.

Though I pass through valleys of deep darkness, I shall not fear–because the Lord, my Defender, is with me.

His rod corrects me, His staff directs me– they are my comfort.

He sets a royal table before me, even in the presence of adversaries. He anoints me– His Oracle–with fresh oil; my cup overflows with revelation, favor, and abundance.

Surely, goodness and mercy pursue me continually, And I shall dwell, abide, and minister in the house of the Lord–forever.

AMEN.

ORACLE OF THE LORD

ORACLE

OF THE

LORD

The world was created by the Word of God. God's Words move swiftly with purpose. He commanded they were created!

"So shall my word be that goes out from my mouth; it shall not return to me empty, but it shall accomplish that which I purpose and shall succeed in the thing for which I sent it".

(ISAIAH 55:11 ESV)

Printed and published in the United States of America.

By

Digital Publishing of Florida, Inc

Oldsmar, FL 34677

ISBN: 978-1-962929-31-8

First Edition.

www.perfectloveffl.com

Table Of Contents

Introduction

Glory to God Almighty

Word of God endures forever. It is a lamp unto my feet and a light unto my path. The law of the LORD is perfect, converting the soul; the testimony of the LORD is sure, making wise the simple" (Psalm 19:7). "Oracle of the LORD" is not merely a book; it is a testament to the power and potency of God's Word. It is a call to reverence, a call to obedience, and a call to intimacy with God. May the words in the book resonate in the depths of souls, igniting passion for truth and hunger for sincere words of God. Every verse, in every story, in every prophecy, within Oracle of the LORD reveals consistence power in God's word.

Show Forth God's Glory

Showing Forth God's Glory is the ultimate purpose behind the Oracle of God. The words within this book are drawn from the scriptures, revelations and rhema words of God. The book goes deeper into the profound power of Word of God and the impact it has on humanity. "The LORD of hosts hath sworn, saying, surely as I have thought, so shall it come to pass; and as I have purposed, so shall it stand." (Isaiah 14:24)

God magnifies His Word more than His Name. This reveals the incomparable power inherent in the Word of

God. God's word expresses God's will and intentions. It carries significance that surpasses even the exaltation of His name. This elevates the transformative potency of God's Word to a level of paramount importance and emphasizing its efficacy in bringing to life fulfillment of God divine promises.

The book is written to magnify and glorify God through series of declarations, reflections, and scriptural insights. Is all about God and God's word. The book presents a vivid picture of how every aspect of life, no matter how mundane or extraordinary can be expression of God's glory.

I wrote this book not out of an abundance of knowledge of the topic, but simply because God has spoken.
I believe it, I obey and that settles it. I raised God's words above my understanding. Proverbs 3:5-7 says "Trust in the Lord with all your heart and lean not on your own understanding; in all your ways submit to him, and he will make your paths straight. Do not be wise in your own eyes; fear the Lord and shun evil"

The power of words of God is a central theme of "Oracle of the LORD". God's word is a source of divine guidance, wisdom, and transformative influence. There are several chapters and verses that illustrate the power in the word of God. (Genesis 1:1) says God created the heavens and the earth"

God's word brought the entire world into existence, demonstrating the creative and authoritative power of God's word. The Bible is the inspired and authoritative words of God. Word from God reveals God's character, will, and plan for humanity. Word of God refers to the teachings, commands, promises, and revelations given by God. This book contains extract words of God from the bible and revelations.

Journey of Obedience

I embark on a journey of self-discovery and awakening through writing Oracle of the LORD book. I earnestly pray for God's divine backing of His words within this book. The LORD is my pasture and my inspiration to write this book. It is profound truth that the LORD often utilizes the seemingly foolish things to confirm His wisdom. God sometimes chooses to manifest His mighty power through ordinary individuals. Who would have anticipated that God would select a young girl like Mary to be the mother of our LORD and Savior, Jesus Christ? Mary was but a young girl when the Angel of God brought her good tidings, revealing to her what seemed impossible to mortal. God in His infinite wisdom knows precisely how to convey messages through any vessel.

In obedient to God, I convey the awesome power in God's word through "Oracle of the LORD" book. "Oracle of the LORD "is absolutory about one word I heard from God. "Be an Oracle of God" "Say thou Saith" God appeared by His word and His word is always correct. This is what this book is about. The Almighty God steadfastly affirms His word and brings to fruition the message dispensed through His messengers.

Call to Obedience

Fundamentally, obedience is the driving force behind my writing "Oracle of the LORD. "Thus says the Lord" I write because God says so. I have no knowledge and the ability to write a book, but I am completely working in obedient to God's word. It's not simply a choice, but an irresistible urge and a profound stirring deep within the soul that compels me to proclaim the words of God. I absolutely acknowledged God and depends on His divine guidance and inspiration to write Oracle of the LORD.

Drawing from my personal experiences and encounters, I have unwavering commitment to following God's clear command. Although, there are sometimes moments of doubt and challenges like in times of Abraham and those who walked in obedience to God. Such moments of doubt will not hinder God from bringing His word to fulfillments. That is why perseverance is encouraged and the transformative power of surrendering to Christ and God's purpose can never be over emphasized.

With every step forward, I endeavor to honor the essence of my being, to live a life that reflects beauty, love, and expression of God's Glory. It is not for me to proclaim my own greatness, but rather to reflect the qualities that God has called upon me to embody. Yet, amidst of external voices, I find refuge in the knowledge that my worth is not determined by worldly standards but by God Almighty.

"Oracle of the LORD" serves as a vessel, emphasizing the truthful God's word as instructed. Each word and each sentence in this book become the canvas of divine revelation of God's beauty and majesty. Readers are encouraged to behold the power of redemption through Jesus Christ. Not by strength but by faith.

Oracle of the LORD

O LORD Almighty, God of Heaven and Earth, illuminate your words meaningfully in the heart of readers. Help them pay attention to your word, not the author. LORD grant readers the desire to experience truth and sincere meaning of your word through this book. In Jesus Name Amen.

Within the pages of Oracle of the LORD, is a journey to discover the enduring power and significance of God's words. Humans stand as God's greatest priority. God's word is steadfast which highlights the enduring and unchanging quality of God's Word. While words of human-beings may fluctuate due to circumstances beyond human control or other reasons, God's word stand firm and steadfast in all situations. Isaiah 40:8 says, "The grass withers and the flowers fall, but the word of God endures forever."

God's word comprises God's will and guidance for humanity. Isaiah 55:11, emphasizes the effectiveness of

God's word, highlighting its power and reliability. "So is my word that goes out from my mouth: It will not return to me empty but will accomplish what I desire and achieve the purpose for which I sent it." The word that goes out from God's mouth cannot return void but must accomplish that which it is sent for. This fundamental truth underscores the potency and effectiveness of God's divine words.

The Bible, as a powerful tool, serves as a compass aligning hearts and minds with God's will. John1:1, "In the beginning was the Word, and the Word was with God, and the Word was God". Hebrews 4:12: "The word of God is living and active, sharper than any two-edged sword." Genesis 11:6 "And the LORD said, Behold the people is one and they have one language; and this they begin to do: and now nothing will be restrained from them, which they have imagined to do."

Oracle of the LORD book acknowledged the limitations of human words and counsels. In contrast, the counsel and words from God Almighty have been affirmed to never fail. Delighting in God's words and meditating on the true words of God regularly is a pathway to knowing God; akin to a tree planted by the rivers of water consistently yielding fruits in all seasons. The promise extends to every aspect of life, Spirit, Soul, and Body.

Oracle of the LORD serves as an exploration of the Oracle's journey to discovering God's purpose. This book is a call to action, encouraging readers to seek opportunities to manifest God's glory in everything and spread love and kindness through the power of God's word. Not by power but through the faith in awesome Savior Jesus Christ. Oracle of the LORD acknowledges challenges sometimes faced by God's vessels. Oracle of the LORD is guided by divine purpose and fueled by the power of God's word which stands as a beacon of light and hope. The charge is clear: declare God's words for they are destined to accomplish the purpose for which they are sent.

Trusting God

Reflecting on heartfelt expression by king David "Thank you, Jesus, for not forsaking me" reflects a deep gratitude for the faithfulness of Christ. It acknowledges the unwavering presence of the Savior, Jesus Christ who in times of trial and triumph has remained a constant source of strength and guidance. This gratitude is rooted in the acknowledgment that Jesus in His love and mercy has been a faithful companion never abandoning the one who seeks refuge in Him.

I express profound gratitude for the interplay between obedience to God's commandments, the redemption found in Christ, and the transformative power of His Words. It is a testament to a life anchored in faith, guided by divine principles, and enriched by the continuous presence of Jesus, the source of life and eternal hope.

Ephesians 4:23 KJV speaks to the continual process of allowing the Holy Spirit to reshape thoughts and attitudes. "And be renewed in the spirit of your mind. Instead let the spirit renew your thoughts and attitudes. Put on your new nature, created to be like God truly righteous and holy. "Oracle of the LORD" recognizes the transformative power of renewing the mind. It is a call to shed the old nature and embrace the new, one that mirrors the righteousness and holiness of God.

Oracle of God inspires readers to embark on their own journeys of faith, obedience, and divine revelation for God's glory for "His Name Sake" "His Name Sake" stands as a testament to the transformative power of God's love and the profound impact of life in obedience to God's word and purpose. God the Father, the Son, and Holy Spirit continue speaking in various ways.

Oracle seeks this renewal as an integral part of embodying the God's message, understanding that a transformed mind aligns with God's purpose. Every word in this book forms a foundation from the scripture.

Scripture is a guiding trust, action, remembrance, and renewal of heart and hope. The verse from the scripture serves as a pillar supporting the Oracle's journey in delivery the divine messages align with God's purpose. Oracle of the LORD understands the significance of living in accordance with divine principles, recognizing that obedience to God's commandments is a pathway to connecting to God and aligning with His purpose.

Words of God is able to keep soul safe in Christ and grant salvation found in relationship with Jesus Christ. Oracle acknowledges the redemptive power of Christ's sacrifice, understanding that through faith and obedience, the soul finds refuge, protection, and strength. Jesus Christ gave life and access to mankind into God's Words. This activates the transformative power of revelation and relationship with Christ.

Oracle recognizes that through Christ, not only is the soul safeguarded, but life itself is infused with purpose and meaning. Access to the Words of God whether through scripture or personal revelation becomes a source of guidance, wisdom, and divine connection. Oracle understands the privilege of having access to the teachings of God's words which illuminate the path to righteousness and eternal life. Studying the word of God creates greater relationships with God. The words of God are truth and food for life and daily living.

Embracing Oracle of the LORD

Acknowledging imperfection, I find solace in the ongoing journey of faith. It is within this imperfect pilgrimage that the inspiration for this book took root. A quiet but resolute conviction reaffirmed within me: "Christie, be my Oracle; Say Thou Saith." It was this divine prompting that emboldened me to put pen to paper, sharing the profound and powerful Words of God.

As I wrote in earlier paragraph, I wrote this book not out of an abundance of knowledge on the topic, but simply because God has spoken. I believe and obeyed God's words. That settles it. The words within this book are drawn from the scriptures and the rhema words of God. Every statement in the oracle stands as a powerful testament to the authority in God's words.

Have I comprehended all of God's words? No. Have I faithfully acted upon every directive from God? No. Have all the promises God made to me come to pass? Not yet. Nevertheless, I find solace in the assurance that God cannot lie. I firmly believe that His words are true and whatever God's word says, is so. If God says it, is so, it remains so for eternity. Nothing could alter it, if the word originated from God. God's words or words of God are opulent script possessing endless meaning and enduring forever. Certain things may be deemed impossible by human standards, but with God all things are possible.

In the pursuit of God's glory, I find my motivation deeply rooted in the unwavering trust and faith I hold in the divine trinity of God the Father, Son, and Holy Spirit. My sense of obedience is not merely a compliance with religious duty but a response to a profound instruction from God. The belief that God can convey a message through any vessel or channel underscores the omnipotence and omnipresence of the Almighty God.

I firmly assert that the authority of God's words transcends any other power in existence. This conviction forms the bedrock of my Christian journey. Is a constant reminder that in God guidance, there is an unparalleled richness and reward awaiting those who diligently and faithfully follow Christ even by faith. Studying the Bible becomes a transformative experience; a direct line of communication with God where wisdom and guidance found within its verses shapes understanding of God's Divine plan for humanity.

The excerpt from 1 Peter 4:11 serves as a beacon, illuminating the path of writing, reading, speaking and ministering in harmony with oracles of the LORD. Its indicates the urge individual ability to operate within the abilities bestowed by God. It is an embodiment of humility and a recognition of divine empowerment, emphasizing that every act of service should ultimately glorify God through Jesus Christ.

Oracle of the LORD is a manifesto for embracing and living according to the profound words of God. It serves as a guide to acknowledge the transcendent power and wisdom within God's words. The Bible verse quoted stands as a timeless principle, challenging all readers to speak and minister in a manner that brings unequivocal glory to God.

I hope this will inspire readers to embrace the transformation of God's guidance. Keeping the commandments of God as a fundamental aspect of life dedicated to following the will of the Almighty God. This commitment involves adhering to the moral and spiritual guidelines laid out in the words of God.

May this book inspire a deeper connection to Christ, the Author and Finisher of our faith and foster a relentless pursuit Jesus Christ the Savior of the Whole World. Readers of this book are invited to examine the words of God in the scripture, to search it out, and to proclaim the truth contained within. The following chapter focuses on the ultimate purpose behind Oracle of the LORD.

Chapter 1: Faith-Filled Exploration

The world was created by the Word of God, whose words move swiftly and with purpose. He sends forth His word, and it melts away all obstacles. There will be a fulfillment of everything God has spoken, for His words carry the power to bring all things to pass. Luke 1: 45 "And blessed is she that believed: for there shall be a performance of those things which were told from the Lord." The Word of God is the message of Christ, a testimony about Him, and the evidence of His truth.

Self-Discovery

In Navigating Self-Discovery, I discover the intricacies of profound exploration into the depths of my belief in Jesus Christ. Adding a personal touch of faith, I share insights from my own understanding, rhema, what God says, and from my own experience reflecting on pivotal moments that shaped my character to embrace the Truth. Oracle of the LORD unfolds with the acknowledgment that God's instruction to everyone is the truth, fair for all, and for the good of everyone.

Navigate God's Word

Oracle of the LORD is a living testimony of witnessing Christ and expressing God's Glory. Christians are called to be living witnesses of Jesus Christ through their lives embodying the teachings of the scriptures. Christians are called to exemplify and testify to the life and teachings of Jesus Christ through their actions and lives.

Navigating the complexities of existence, actions and choices serve as a testament to the Lord Jesus Christ.

This book is not a declaration of perfection but an invitation to embrace the journey of becoming living testimonies. It is an exploration of the divine transformation through imperfections and profound truth witnesses of Christ. Every life become a canvas on which God's prophetic words are beautifully reflected. In recognizing my own imperfections, I became a vessel for God's message. Encouraging myself using Philippians 2:13 KJV "For it is God which worketh in us both to will and to do of his good pleasure."

Oracle of the LORD understands the profound truth in Ephesians 1:17 KJV. "That the God of our Lord Jesus Christ, the Father of glory, may give unto you the spirit of wisdom and revelation in the knowledge of him" This is the acknowledgement that God is actively at work, shaping both His people's desires and actions according to His divine purpose. As the Oracle endeavors to fulfill the divine calling, this verse serves as a constant reminder that the motive, motivation and action is rooted in God's good pleasure. Oracle leans on this assurance recognizing that the power to carry out God's will emanate from the Almighty himself.

Another reference verse is Revelation 19:10, "At this I fell at his feet to worship him. But he said to me, "Don't do that! I am a fellow servant with you and with your brothers and sisters who hold to the testimony of Jesus. Worship God! For it is the Spirit of prophecy who bears testimony to Jesus." This verse unveils the transformative power of bearing witness for Christ. According to Isaiah 26:4 KJV. "Trust ye in the LORD forever: for in the LORD JEHOVAH is everlasting strength." This verse from Isaiah emphasizes the enduring nature of trusting in God's word.

Oracle of the LORD is an invitation to put trust in the God's word, not just temporarily but at all times. Oracle of the LORD recognizes that true strength; the kind of strength that surpasses the transient strengths of the word of Almighty God. This trust forms the bedrock of Oracle's journey anchoring in the unwavering strength found in God alone.

Reflection on God's eternal truth; Jesus Christ. God's words are inherently prophetic, carrying the weight of divine wisdom and foresight. It is with this understanding that I humbly present the insights within the pages of Oracle of the LORD as humble attempt to convey the profound truth in God's Word.

Isaiah 43:26 KJV

"Put me in remembrance: let us plead together: declare thou, that thou mayest be justified." In Oracle of God's journey, the directive from Isaiah encourages dialogue with the Almighty. God invites the Oracle to remember and declare God's promises. The Oracle understands the importance of reaffirming God's faithfulness to align with God's words and promises.

The Word

The Heaven is created through God's creative command. Everything God created manifested through God's word and His Spirit. God's creations are attributed to the Almighty God's divine words. Words of God transform lives. All of God's words are profitable and useful. The Word of God is impartial, consistent, perfect and righteous. There is no partiality, contradiction, and unrighteous judgment in God's Word. God's words encompass various terms, each with its own distinctions. Here are a few key terms to words of God:

1. **Logos**

   The term "Logos" is of Greek origin and is used in the Gospel of John to refer to Jesus Christ as the Word of God incarnate. It represents the divine eternal expression of God.

2. **Rhema**

   Rhema refers to the spoken or revealed word of God. It is often used to emphasize a specific, personal, or timely message from God to an individual. The distinction between Logos and Rhema is that Logos is the general eternal word of God while

Rhema is a specific revealed word for a particular person or situation.

3. **Scripture/Bible**

   The Bible is the written word of God. It is divided into the Old Testament and the New Testament and contains various genres, including historical narratives, poetry, prophecy, and revelation.

The Bible is true, reliable, and inspired by God. It is not the opinion of men but the truth, reliable, and consistent words of God. What makes the Bible unique is that it is written by many authors. It is the same in every nation and is always consistent, correct, and current.

4. **Prophetic Words**

   Prophetic words are messages directly from God, often delivered through prophets. In some Christian traditions, individuals with the gift of prophecy may receive and convey specific words, guidance, or revelations from God.

5. **General Revelation**

   General revelation refers to the idea that God's existence and attributes are revealed through nature, the created world, and the order of the earth. This is distinct from specific, personal messages (Rhema) and the written scriptures (Logos).

6. **Preached Word/Sermons**
    The preaching of God's word is a common practice in Christian worship. Pastors and preachers deliver sermons to convey and explain the teachings found in the Bible for the edification and instruction of the congregation.

The terms and concepts may vary in emphasis or interpretation among different Christian denominations and traditions. Studying and understanding the various aspects of God's words contribute to richer comprehension of God's word and Christian growth.

Sometimes believers find themselves confronted with profound questions about God's word and reliability. As the Author of "Oracle of the LORD," I honestly and humbly acknowledging the complexities and mysteries of God's word. The Holy Bible is esteemed by millions worldwide as the written word of God. Yet, even within the pages of the Bible, there are diversity of genres, perspectives, and historical contexts. Therefore, there is a need for people to recognize that while every word may not be direct from God, the overarching message of love, redemption, and guidance remains steadfast and true. "Has God said it and failed to perform it?" No.

Channels of God's Word

In the journey of faith in Jesus Christ as the LORD and SAVIOR, understanding how God communicates with humanity is pivotal. While the scriptures serve as a cornerstone, God's word manifests through diverse and numerous channels, each carrying its unique resonance. The effectiveness of these diverse sources offers profound insights into the nature of powerful God's words. The Scripture as the Foundation stands as the bedrock of divine revelation, offering timeless truths and guiding principles.

Through diligent study and reflection, believers glean wisdom, guidance, and solace from God's word. The effectiveness of the scriptures lies in the ability to transcend time and culture, speaking and piercing directly to human soul across generations. For some, the voice of God resonates audibly, cutting through the noise of everyday life with unmistakable clarity.

Such encounters while rare are profound and life-transforming, leaving indelible imprints on the hearts and minds of those who experience it. Exploring the effectiveness of audible voices requires discernment and deep openness to the presence of Holy Spirit.

Still small voice within often describe as the witness of the heart serves as a gentle whisper guiding towards the mind of God. This inner knowing borne of communion with the LORD offers reassurance, direction, and affirmation in times of uncertainty. Understanding the effectiveness of this subtle yet powerful channel requires cultivating a sensitive spirit attuned to the presence of Holy Spirit.

Through the prophetic voice; Throughout history God has spoken through prophets; men and women endowed with a unique capacity to hear and convey divine messages. The effectiveness of prophetic utterances lies in the ability to challenge, inspire, and edify people or communities. However, discernment is essential as not all who wear the mantle of prophecy speak to and hear from the Holy God's authority.

The language of dreams. Dreams have long been recognized as a conduit for divine communication with God. Insights, warnings, and revelations to those who heed their messages. The effectiveness of dream interpretation lies in deciphering the symbolic language through which God speaks. This is unraveling layers of meaning and significance. Cultivating receptive posture to the language of dreams opens portals to profound encounters with God.

As reveal by "Oracle of the Lord" each thread whether drawn from the scriptures, audible voices, witness of the heart, the prophetic voice, or the language of dreams contributes to the richness of God's word. Understanding the effectiveness of these diverse channels requires humility, discernment, unwavering love and commitment to seeking the truth faithfully.

1. John 1:1 KJV

"In the beginning was the Word, and the Word was with God, and the Word was God." This profound verse is from the Gospel of John which is the fourth book in the New Testament. In this verse, "the Word" is a reference to Jesus. It emphasizes that Jesus exists from the very beginning. Jesus was with God and still with God. Jesus is in fact divine (God). This verse is fundamental to Christian belief in the divinity of Jesus Christ and the Holy Trinity; Father, Son (the Word), and Holy Spirit.

2. Psalm 33:4 KJV

"For the word of the LORD is right; And all his works are done in truth." This verse is from the Book of Psalms in the Old Testament. The verse highlights the righteousness and truthfulness of the Word of God. God's word is reliable, just, and trustworthy. The emphasis is on the moral and ethical perfection of God's word. His commands and teachings are inherently right and truthful.

3. Isaiah 55:11 KJV

"So shall my word be that goeth forth out of my mouth: it shall not return unto me void, but it shall accomplish that which I please, and it shall prosper in the thing whereto I sent it." This verse is from the Book of Isaiah in the Old Testament. Here, God is expressing the effectiveness and power of His Word. When God speaks, His Word is like a force that goes out and accomplishes what He desires. Words from God will not be empty or in vain but able to achieve its intended purpose. This emphasizes the authority and efficacy of God's Word.

These verses collectively convey the importance and power of the word of God. The word refers to the divine nature of Jesus Christ and emphasizes its righteousness, truthfulness, and effectiveness. The potency of God's word is a cornerstone that transcends the limitations of human comprehension. This underscores the steadfast nature of God's promises. Unlike human pledges that may succumb to unforeseen circumstances.
Promises from God bear the impenetrable seal of omniscience. God's knowledge understands the end from the beginning.

Redemption Revelation
Within the pages of *'Oracle of the LORD,'* places emphasis for those who seek to understand the depths of God's word, mercy, and grace. Oracle of the LORD invites readers into the heart of God's redemptive plan. The suffering of Jesus Christ, whose sacrifice heralds a new dawn of salvation for humanity. As the prophet's words confirmed through the ages. Unveiling the profound mystery of Christ's atoning work and the unparalleled love of the Creator for His creation.

Loving and Serving God for Who He Is:
First, the reason to love and serve God should indeed be rooted in who God is. God, by His very nature, is worthy of love, honor, and worship. God is the Creator of all things, the source of life, and the embodiment of goodness, justice,

and truth. Because of these attributes, God deserves love and service simply for being God—holy, sovereign, and perfect. Loving God for who He is acknowledges His greatness and majesty, beyond what He has done for us personally.

Knowing God is loving and serving God for what He has done and what he continues to do. God's actions, specifically the redemption provided through Jesus Christ offers another compelling reason to love and serve God. The sacrifice of Christ on the cross is a demonstration of God's immense love and mercy. It shows His willingness to forgive sins, restore relationships, and offer eternal life. This redemptive act provides a personal, tangible reason to respond with love, gratitude, and service. This is because God through Jesus Christ has redeemed believers. The grace and mercy of God is an inspiration to love and serve God wholeheartedly.

Loving God for who He is, naturally leads to gratitude for what He has done and what He will continue doing. Likewise, appreciating the redemption offered by Christ helps believers to see more clearly the character and nature of God. The love for God should not be conditional or based only on what He gives, but it should also be deeply personal, arising from an understanding of His character and His acts of grace.

Ultimately, the reason to love and serve God is both because of His nature as the all-powerful, all-loving Creator, and because of the redemptive work of Christ, which brings love into a personal and transformative reality for each believer. These motivations together create a holistic understanding of why God is worthy of love and service.

Think about this declaration for a moment "He was taken from prison and from judgment" It speaks of Christ's mission. Though He was innocent, He willingly submitted Himself to the chains of human suffering and the verdict of death. Yet, in His obedience, He shattered the bonds of sin and death, setting captives free and granting hope to the hopeless.

As "Oracle of the LORD" proclaims the generation of the redeemed, it becomes a living testament to the transformative power of God's grace. Those who have been touched by His mighty hand are not merely spectators but active participants in the salvation. Their lives become a living testament to the miraculous work of God, declaring His praises to all. Words of God stand as a timeless testament to the unfathomable depths of God's love and the transformative power of redemption.

Chapter 2: Understanding God's Word

Relationship and Discernment

The Word of God as described in various scriptures is depicted as a living, quick, sharp, and powerful entity that holds unparalleled significance in the lives of believers. God's word serves as lively oracles given to humanity. Word of God possess the ability to pierce into the deepest soul and spirit. Word of God can pierce into the deepest soul and spirit emphasizes its profound impact on individuals' spiritual lives. It is not merely a collection of teachings but a dynamic force that interacts with and transforms believers. By engaging deeply with the Word, people can experience personal growth, moral clarity, and a closer relationship with God. "Word of God possesses the ability to pierce into the deepest soul and spirit" is a powerful statement.

Omniscient and Omnipotent

God being the omniscient and omnipotent entity, possesses an unparalleled awareness of the obstacles and challenges that may impede the fulfillment of His promises. The story of Abraham and Sarah stands as a testament to the profundity of words of God. God assured the elderly couple that they would conceive a child, it defied the conventions of human biology and circumvented the constraints of their advanced age.

This divine promise served as an unequivocal affirmation that God's word operates beyond the limitations of the natural order.

Impossibilities

The inherent power in God's word lies in its ability to transform the seemingly impossible into tangible reality. Humanly impossible scenarios, such as Abraham and Sarah bearing a child in their old age are not exceptions but rather exemplifications of the God's word and capability to supersede natural limitations. God's promise is not contingent upon the feasibility discernible to human reasoning; rather it hinges on the absolute authority of the One who declares it.

The Infallibility God's Words

Unlike human promises that may falter due to unforeseen circumstances, changing minds, or a lack of capacity to fulfill, God's word is infallible. The very nature of God ensures a steadfast commitment to His Word. He is not bound by the constraints of times or hindrances by external forces. God's self-existent and unchanging nature establishes a foundation for His words to resonate with unwavering truth.

The Essence of God's Sovereignty

The omnipotence and sovereignty of God distinguish His word from humans. God's autonomy enables Him to act in accordance with His will, unrestricted by external influences. In contrast to human fallibility, God is the epitome of reliability.

His promises are not contingent upon human merit, circumstance, or probability; rather, they emanate from a divine source that transcends the temporal and finite. The statement that "Has God said it and failed to perform it?" captures the essence of the indomitable power inherent in God's word. The statement exemplified through the scripture, serve as beacons of hope and assurance for believers. God's word stands as an irrefutable testament to the omnipotence, omniscience, and unwavering commitment of the Creator to fulfill His promises.

In a world fraught with uncertainties, the constancy of God's word remains an anchor for those who seek solace and assurance beyond the realm of human understanding. Words of God are infallible and carries enduring truth. God's word carries authority that is inspiring. Words of God are ultimate authority providing guidance and commandments to follow without question. Infallibility words of God confirms that God's words are absolutely truth and carries wisdom. God's words are not only historical but also living words that are relevance in shaping lives; beliefs, practices, and standards.

Consistent Truth in God's Word

God's word is the ultimate truth. This consistency is divinely orchestrated with historical events continually affirming the veracity and stability of God's word. As stated in Psalm 119:89, "Forever, O Lord, thy word is settled in heaven." This underlines that God's promises, as Paul affirms in 2 Corinthians 1:20, are always "yes" and "amen."

"For all the promises of God in him are yea, and in him Amen unto the glory of God by us."

The importance of engaging with scripture is highlighted in 1 Timothy 4:13, which encourages believers to devote themselves to reading. This engagement is critical because anything inconsistent with the scripture may be unreliable. Paul's assertion in Galatians 1:12, his message was received directly from God and not from man, further emphasizes the divine origin and authority of God's word.

The Holy Spirit, referred to as the Spirit of Truth in John 16:13, is believed to guide believers into all truth, reinforcing the consistency found in God's word. Sanctification which recognizes the divine inspiration through Jesus Christ solidifies this consistency of God's Word.

Ezekiel 37:7-10 exemplifies the power and reliability of God's word. The prophet obedience to God's command brought life and unity to dry bones, symbolizing the revitalizing power of God's word. The verse illustrates how God's blessings manifest, not based on hearsay, but on the reveal truth and revelation.

The word of God stands as a testament to divine consistency and reliability, offering foundation of truth that humans can depend on throughout history and into the future.

Incarnate Transformation

John 1:14, "And the Word became flesh and dwelt among us," a revelation unfolds showcasing the unparalleled power embedded in God's word. This transformed nature of God's word surpasses other words, and it can sometime take on human form, embodying unfailing love, grace, and truth. The scripture confirmed with a resounding truth in God's Word. His words are not mere collection of syllables but dynamic force that took on tangible existence. The incarnation of the Word, becoming flesh, marks a pivotal moment in the redemptive power through Jesus Christ and the Holy Spirit. Holy Spirit is the hand that touches human in an extraordinary way. "It is the spirit that quickeneth; the flesh profiteth nothing: the words that I speak unto you, they are spirit, and they are life." (John 6:63 KJV) This verse is part of Jesus discourse after feeding the 5,000 and walking on water where He speaks about being the Bread of Life.

Key Phrases

"It is the spirit that quickeneth," The word "quickeneth" means to give life. Jesus is emphasizing that it is the Holy Spirit that gives spiritual life and vitality.

"The words that I speak unto you, they are spirit, and they are life," Jesus declares word of God are not ordinary words but are imbued with the power of the Holy Spirit.

Chapter 3: Distinguish God's Word

By His word

God's Words are effective, reliable and powerful. The effectiveness of God's word goes as far when spoken through His chosen vessels. It serves as a reminder that God's promises are sure, and His messages are reliable. Just as Samuel's words were fulfilled without fail, so are the promises and prophecies from God chosen vessels. It reinforces the importance of heeding the word of God and recognizing the authority behind it.

God's words are not empty or in vain. God's words carry the weight of divine truth and uphold by the power of God. Oracle of the LORD emphasizes the centrality of God's word as the creative force. "And Samuel grew, and the Lord was with him, and did let none of his words fall to the ground." This verse is a testament to the reliability and effectiveness of the word of God. 1 Samuel 3:19 is the story of Samuel who as a young boy was called by God to serve as a prophet. The verse describes Samuel's growth and the divine presence that accompanies him throughout his life. "And did let none of his words fall to the ground" Samuel was under the guidance of God. It amplifies the authority and trustworthiness of God's word conveys by God through His chosen medium.

In 1 Samuel 1:11, the fervent prayer of Hannah, a woman deeply distressed by her inability to conceive a child prayed and God intervened. In her desperation, she makes a solemn vow to the Lord, saying, "O Lord of hosts, if thou wilt indeed look on the affliction of thine handmaid, and remember me and not forget thine handmaid, but wilt give unto thine handmaid a man child, then I will give him unto the Lord all the days of his life and there shall no razor come upon his head." This verse underscores the potency and efficacy of the power inherent in the Word of God.

Hannah's prayer isn't just a desperate plea; it's a powerful call of faith and trust in the Almighty God. She believes that if God grants her request, she will dedicate her child to His service. This is a fact that illustrates when desires are aligned with God's will and expressed through sincere prayer, God has the power to bring it fulfillment. Hannah's faith isn't in vain for in due time, she conceived and gave birth to a son whom she named Samuel.

Similarly, in Daniel 10:11, here is another instance where the reliability of God's Word is emphasized. Daniel was visited by an angel who comes in response to his prayers. The angel reassures Daniel by saying, "O Daniel, a man greatly beloved, understand the words that I speak unto thee and stand upright: for unto thee am I sent. And when he had spoken this word unto me, I stood trembling."

God's Word is not only reliable but also powerful. The presence of the angel and the assurance of his words bring comfort and strength to Daniel.

Both 1st Samuel 1:11 and Daniel 10:11 highlight the unwavering faithfulness of God to His promises and the effectiveness of His Word when earnestly declared and believed. When we call upon the Lord with sincerity and trust, He hears our prayers and acts according to His will, demonstrating His power and faithfulness.

God's word is not merely a linguistic expression but an active and dynamic agent of God's divine power. In Genesis, God speaks the world into existence revealing the authority and efficacy of His word. Psalm 33:6 "By the word of the Lord the heavens were made, their starry host by the breath of his mouth. This verse is a poetic and inspiring declaration of the creative power of God's word. It vividly confirms the origin and divine agency behind the creation of the heavens and the earth.

Unshakable God's Word

In a world filled with uncertainties, one constant that remains continually is unwavering power of God's word. The Oracle of the LORD book serves as a profound testament to sovereign and authority embedded in every word of God. Word of God is a guiding lamp which illuminating heart. "Thy word is a lamp unto my feet, and a light unto my path." These words confirm the profound wisdom that God's words are not just an intellectual pursuit but a source of guidance and direction in daily journey

God's Word vs Men's Word

God's Word

God's word is a possessive form, indicating that the words belong to God. God own His word and God is the sole authorship of His words. Words of God are God spoken or expressed by God in a broader sense, including commandments, guidance, or any form of communication believed to come directly from the God the Father, Son, and Holy Spirit.

Words of God

Words of God typically refers to the utterances, teachings, or messages that are attributed to God. It encompasses various forms of communication from God, such as reading from the scriptures or divine revelations.

In this context, "words of God" are the expressions or statements that are believed to originate from God's divine sources. Human's words are unlike God's word. God's word transcends time and circumstance, human words may potentially fail but God's word never fail.

Timeless Relevance Word

Zachariah 1:6 encourages believers to embrace the enduring God's Words, and commandments. God's words have profound impacts on existence. Zachariah 1:6 (ESV)"But my words and my statutes, which I commanded my servants the prophets, did they not overtake your fathers? So, they repented and said, 'As the Lord of hosts purposed to deal with us for our ways and deeds, so has he dealt with us."

This verse serves as a reminder of the unchanging power inherent in God's words and statutes. It unveils a divine guidance which can be trace back through history. As God commanded His servants, the prophets to proclaim His truths in His words through time, reaching even the forefathers. From generation to generation, the impact of God's words remains consistent. They are not mere relics of the past but living active of divine wisdom of God. God's words overtake the forefathers' word. God words lead to repentance Introspection and timeless. God's words are not confined to the pages of ancient scripture; they are living forces, relevant and potent in every season. His commandments, spoken through prophets of old continues, thereby inviting people to repentance and inspiring in alignment with God's purpose.

God's word has the capacity to transform and lead people towards God's will. Zachariah 1:6 is enduring promise that God's words are not bound by time or circumstance. They are guiding lights which offers wisdom and insight to navigate complexities journeys. The beauty of Zachariah 1:6 lies in its revelation of the timeless relevance of God's word. Is an invitation to reflect on the divine powerful word and wisdom in God's word. Some Believers often witness the transformative power that leads to repentance and turning away from one's own ways to embrace the divine purpose through God's Words or Words of God.

Everlasting God's Words

God's words are living, powerful, and enduring forever. The verse underscores the consistent and purposeful nature of God's will towards humanity. an enduring love that seeks the best and calls to life. A reflection of God eternal truths. This underscores the consistent and purposeful power of God's word. God's words are enduring words that seek the best of humanity.

Living

The living nature of God's words is an ongoing relevance that transcends temporal boundaries. God's words are living because they have the ability to breathe life into hearts and souls. God's Word are dynamic, not confined to a specific era or culture. God's word possesses the inherent capacity to inspire, guide, and bring positive change to humanity.

Powerful

The power of God's words lies in the ability to create, shape, and sustain. It is a power that goes beyond human comprehension, influencing both the seen and unseen aspects of existence. The transformative impact of the Word is evident of God almighty. Words that provide solace during challenges. God's word offers solution in times of distress. It serves as moral compass and provides righteous living.

Enduring Forever

The enduring God's words signifies the timeless relevance and unwavering significance throughout the ages.

Unlike human philosophies or worldly knowledge that may fade with time. God's words stand as an eternal foundation. God's word remains constant in a world marked by changes and diversity offering sources of guidance and wisdom that endures across generations.

The living, powerful, and enduring God's words reflects the ability to transcend the limitations of time and space, providing sources of eternal guidance and strength for those who seek the Word for nourishment and understanding.

The Word of God is a living, powerful, and enduring force that brings joy, discernment, and assurance to the hearts of believers. It pierces through the depths of the human soul, revealing the thoughts and intents of the heart. Believers are called to embrace and meditate on God's words, recognizing the purity and distinguishing it from deceptive teachings. God's word must align with sources of enduring truth and DeVine wisdom. Sometimes, to experience transformative power of the living Word of God requires faith.

Authority and Sovereignty

Authority and Sovereignty of God emphasizes the sovereignty and authority of God. When actions are undertaken "for His Name's Sake," it signifies that God's interventions and plans are driven by His own authority and divine will. It confirms that God acts in accordance with His character, righteousness, and glory.

Fulfillment of Promises

Throughout the Bible, God made numerous promises to His people. The fulfillment of these promises is often explicitly stated to be "for His Name's Sake." This implies that God's faithfulness and commitment to His word are intrinsically tied to the preservation and exaltation of His name.

Chapter 4: Compass and Map

Powerful God's Words

Proverbs 3:5-6, says, "Trust God with all your heart and rely not on your own understanding." This passage serves as a foundational principle for believers. It emphasizes the need to trust omnipotent knowledge and power of God's word. This is because it is only God that knows all. The transformative power of keeping and walking according to God's Word is indisputable. Adherence to the Words of God upholds and strengthens the foundation of those who have faith in words of God. Faith in words of God will ultimately leads to good prosperity of soul, spirit, and body. The threads of faith are woven with the profound guidance found in the scriptures.

The culmination of the chapters confirms the core meaning of God's Word. The righteousness of God is obtained through faith in Jesus Christ. Faith grants everyone access to the powerful Words of God. It is not limited by social, cultural, or other distinctions. Faith helps to rely on God's word and strength to wait for the manifestation. The Oracle of the LORD affirms that faith is the key that opens the door to receive the transformative and life-giving Words of God.

The scriptures are testament to the multifaceted nature of God's word revealing the inherent strength and power embedded in His words. Drawing inspiration from Psalms 103:18 (KJV), is a reminder that God keeps His covenant with those who remember His commandments and diligently seek to follow God's word. This confirms the covenant that leads to unshakeable foundation upon which faith is anchored.

God's words are elucidated. Words of God can direct believers' path to the right direction. When faced with uncertainty or indecision, relying in words of God becomes encouragement and guidance. There is universality access to God's words by everyone. Everyone has the privilege to seek and find guidance from the word of God.

Drawing from Revelation 22:7 KJV, "Behold, I come quickly: blessed is he that keepeth the sayings of the prophecy of this book." This verse serves as a reminder of the imminent return of Christ and the blessings bestowed upon those who adhere to the Word of God.

Joshua 1:8 KJV. "This book of the law shall not depart out of thy mouth; but thou shalt meditate therein day and night." This verse underscores the transformative power of meditating on God's Word, promising prosperity and good success to those who live according to Words of God. Thereby the Soul, Spirit and Body prosper by deeply reflecting on God's words.

Majesty of His Reign

"The LORD sworn that His thought shall come to pass, and His purpose stands forever." This verse serves as assurance setting the stage for an exploration into the profound God's word. God reigns in Heaven and sits to control the Earth, extends His mercy as a comforting embrace to humanity. History has uncovered the wondrous deeds accomplished through Word of God. From the inception of creation, the counsels of God have proven faithful and truthful to divine purpose that transcends the confines of mortal understanding.

The scriptures are testament to the multifaceted powerful words of God. There are inherent strength and power embedded in God's words. Drawing inspiration from Psalms 103:18 (KJV) is a reminder that God keeps His covenant with those who remember His commandments and diligently seek to follow God's word. This confirms the covenant that leads to unshakeable foundation upon which faith is anchored.

Through moments of trial and triumph, God's promises become an unwavering source of hope and guidance. The transformative power of God's Word goes more than can imagine. The synergy of the eternal Word and the majestic reign of God create things from nothing. God encourages the enduring legacy of His words. The scriptures serve as both a compass and a map, guiding believers through the intricacies of God's voice. God's Word provides wisdom, encouragement, and instruction, offering great rewards and helping grow in faith.

Authority in God's Word

In a world filled with fluctuating ideologies and ever-changing perspectives, the words of God stand as an unwavering pillar of truth. Words of God are not just powerful; they are the very essence of sovereignty and absolute right. God's word aligns with His good pleasure, transcends all human understanding, establishing standards that are unmatched and unparalleled.

The sovereignty of God's word is unassailable, standing firm in the face of any circumstance. God's words remain unaffected. No force in the universe can alter it if God declares it so. God's words are not subject to the whims of time or the capriciousness of mortal minds; rather, they are sufficient, perpetual, and timeless.

God's words is imbued with a moral authority that surpasses human comprehension. God's words are not bound by the limitations of earthly ethics. Words from true God are immortal, existing beyond the confines of mortality. The words that are everlasting endurance through the ages. In a world where trends and opinions evolve, God's word remains relevant across the vast expanse of time.

Unlike fleeting notions that come and go, God's word is not subject to obsolescence. It is in a perpetual state of relevance, an eternal truth that applies to the past, resonates in the present, and extends into the future. In a world that often succumbs to the sway of popular opinion, God's word is not swayed by passing fads.

God's word is and always will be in a state of perpetual trending, never succumbing to the label of being outdated.

The words of God are timeless beacon of truth, an unchanging guide that navigates the complexities of existence. Oracle of the LORD affirms that God's word is always accurate. The immutability makes God's word the supreme and absolute standard which all else is measured. Believers find solace in the constancy of God's word, a refuge that transcends the ebb and flow of temporal concerns.

Unchanging God's Word

In a world marked by constant development and technological advancement, the power of God stands as an immutable force, impervious to the ever-shifting tides of progress. The unyielding nature of God's power emanates from His powerful dynamic words and unchanging consistency as in yesterday, today, and tomorrow. Unlike the ever-evolving words of men which are subject to alteration due to circumstances or shifting perspectives. God's words remain steadfast and unwavering.

God's promises endure, standing as an eternal testament to His faithfulness. The unchanging God's words provides secure foundation, transcend the fleeting nature of worldly developments. The scriptures declare that God magnifies His words above His name. This emphasizes the paramount importance and indomitable authority inherent in God's words.

This elevation of God's words signifies potency that surpasses even the sanctity of His name, underscoring the unparalleled power within God's word.

Genesis chapter one illustrates the creative power of God's words. In the beginning, He created the Heavens and the Earth through the sheer force of His utterances. This manifestation of divine power serves as a testament to the intrinsic potency embedded within every word that proceeds from the mouth of God. The word of the LORD is right; it is a source of truth and righteousness. By the powerful word of the LORD, the heavens and the earth were created.

God's divine words are not only embodying perfect wisdom and justice but also holds the creative force that brought the entire universe into existence. It reassures us of God's omnipotence and the unwavering reliability of His words or promises.

The unchanging power of God's words extends beyond the confines of time, reaching into the eternal. God's promises are not subject to limitations of temporal existence but stand secure for everlasting. In a world where changes are constant, God's steadfastness provides assurance that God's words are not swayed by the transient nature of human affairs.

There is solace and strength in embracing the unchanging powerful words of God. Word of God is a force that transcends the ephemeral trends of human progress, offering timeless source of guidance and assurance. In a world where everything may be subject to development and change, the power of God stands as an eternal constant unwavering beacon of hope and truth.

Divine Precision in God's word

In Daniel 10:11, we find a profound testament to the precision and efficacy of God's word. The verse reads, and he said to me, "O Daniel, man greatly loved, understand the words that I speak to you, and stand upright for now I have been sent to you.' And when he had spoken this word to me, I stood up trembling." This verse captures the essence of precise words from God. From the inception of God's command to its execution.

God's word spark action as seen in the obedience of Daniel. The phrase "at thy word unto thy word I came" confirms the immediacy and unquestionable authority inherent in God's word. Unlike human speech which may be fallible and open to misinterpretation, God's word is infallible and precise.

This highlights the limitations of human understanding in prophesying. "Men prophesy in parts, it is only God that knows the whole," Human comprehension is inherently limited and only God possesses the omniscience required for complete understanding and interpretation of His word.

Oracle of the LORD is central to the theme which is the unwavering accuracy of God's word. Despite the potential for misinterpretation or false proclamation by some individuals, the intrinsic truthfulness and reliability of God's word remain constant. It transcends human error and deception, serving as an immutable foundation of truth in a world fraught with uncertainty and falsehoods.

The essence of Oracle of the LORD book lies in discerning the truthfulness of God's words amidst the myriad interpretations offered by humans. It emphasizes the necessity of aligning one's understanding with the inherent truth of God's word rather than relying solely on human interpretation. Through this, the Oracle of the LORD underscores the significance of discernment and unwavering faith in the face of misleading messages.

Divine Precision in God's word unveiled the Truth in God's Word and invites readers to contemplate the profound implications of Daniel 10:11 and similar passages, urging believers to embrace the inherent accuracy and efficacy of God's word while remaining vigilant against false interpretations and proclamations.

Manifestation of God's Glory

God's words as both fruitful and truthful. In Revelation 3:7, "These are the words of him who is holy and true, who holds the key of David. What he opens no one can shut, and what he shuts no one can open." This verse confirms the unwavering authority and integrity inherent in the divine God's Words. The verse extends to the transformative impact of Word of God. A compelling example is found in the swift change undergone by Saul when he departed from Samuel. The Spirit of God descended upon Saul, prompting him to prophesy alongside other prophets, showcasing the immediate and profound influence of God's words.

Chapter 5: Enduring God's Word

Redemption through Jesus Christ

One of the extraordinary powers of the Word of God is its ability to pierce into the very core of human existence. God's word penetrates the Soul and Spirit, reaching even the marrow, and discerning the thoughts and intent of the heart. In Jeremiah 1:12 says, "I will hasten my word to perform it." This unveils that God's Word is not a passive utterance but dynamic active and efficacious force. There is sense of urgency, purpose, and a commitment from the Almighty to actively bring about the fulfillment of His promises.

Source of Hope

Romans 15:4 (KJV) emphasizes the enduring relevance of the scripture highlighting significant impact of God's word. The verse reads: "For whatsoever things were written aforetime were written for our learning that we through patience and comfort of the scriptures might have hope." This verse confirms the enduring God's Word. God's words contained are not confined to the historical context in which they were written. Instead, they serve as a timeless source of guidance, wisdom, and encouragement for those seek God's will. The reference verse is an invitation to embrace God's words with patience, recognizing that the purpose must surely unfold. It may be gradually or over a time but cannot fail.

"Though it tarries, God's word must surely come to pass". (Habakkuk 2:3) "For the revelation awaits an appointed time; it speaks of the end and will not prove false. Though it lingers, wait for it; it will certainly come and will not delay. "This verse is part of a prophecy given to the prophet Habakkuk. The passage refers to a vision that has been received but hasn't yet been fulfilled. The prophet was told to wait patiently for its fulfillment because even though it might seem to take a long time, it will definitely come to pass according to God's timing.

Though it tarries, "God's word must surely come to pass" It confirms if something seems to be delayed or taking longer than expected, if it's in alignment with God's will, it will inevitably happen. It's a message of patience, faith, and trust in God's timing.

Through patient study of the Words of God, there is deeper understanding of God's plan and purpose. Thereby finding comfort in the eternal truths that transcend the limitations of any era. Moreover, the scriptures are wellspring of hope. The enduring messages of faith, perseverance, and divine providence contained in the Word of God provides comfort when facing challenges and uncertainties. The verse encourages to draw strength and assurance from the scriptures, fostering a resilient hope that transcends the trials of life.

Transformative God's Word

I have witnessed the profound effectiveness of God's power manifested through His Word. There are moments when the circumstances surrounding situations seemed insurmountable and no way through. Words of God often intervene in those very moments.

The transformative power of God's Word is not a mere abstraction; it is a tangible force that can carry people through challenges beyond capacity to overcome. In moments of despair and uncertainty, the reassuring promises in God's words became lifeline guidance with unwavering precision.

Daily, I find myself undergoing a process of transformation and renewal through the inherent power embedded in the words of God. It is not a superficial change but a profound transmutation that transcends the limitations of my own understanding. The transformative nature of God's Word is a testament to its effectiveness in reshaping lives and molding hearts.

Isaiah 46:10, "Declaring the end from the beginning, and from ancient times the things that are not yet done, saying, my counsel shall stand, and I will do all my pleasure" This explain the vastness of God's knowledge, wisdom, and power. It declares that God knows the end from the beginning and from ancient times. He foretells things that are yet to unfold. His counsel remains steadfast.

God accomplishes His purposes with unfailing precision. Isaiah 46:10, serves as a reminder that God's Word is not bound by the constraints of time; rather, it holds the power to shape destinies and orchestrate events according to His divine pleasure.

The omnipotent nature of God's knowledge is not limited to Christianity matters alone. God is aware of all things; He has intimate knowledgeable about every facet of existence. From the intricacies of history to significant theories, God's understanding surpasses human comprehension. His wisdom encompasses the breadth of human knowledge and extends into the boundless realms of the unknown.

In reflecting upon my journey, I am convinced that the effectiveness of God's power is not contingent on human understanding or circumstance. It is an omnipotent force that operates beyond the constraints in the world. Word of God provides hope, guidance, and transformation to humanity. The transformative power of God's Word is an enduring testament to the limitless possibilities that unfold when life and purpose aligned with divine word of God that transcends time and space.

Undisputable Will of God

"God made a decree which shall not pass away," is a declaration that transcends the limitations of time. The statement emphasizes the enduring power in word of God. Words of God are eternal and unchangeable. This illustrates the authoritative power in words from God. The assurance that God's decree shall not pass signifies its permanence and immutability. It speaks to the timeless God's will. God's word remains unaffected by the transient nature of the world. God making a decree that endures forever underscores His supreme authority. It confirms a divine plan and purpose that extends beyond the fluctuations of human circumstances. God's words provide firm foundation of stability in an ever-changing world.

Unalterable decree reflects on the reliability of God's intentions. The assurance God's word will not pass away instills a sense of confidence in the divine wisdom and foresight of the Almighty God. This serves as source of comfort for those navigating the uncertainties of life, offering firm foundation upon which to build faith and trust on. The acknowledgement that God made a decree which shall not pass away is assurance inheritance in word of God.

Words of God provides paths worthy of emulating and a guiding force for ethical and moral living. Thereby providing compass for navigating the complexities of human existence. "God made a decree which shall not pass away" resonates as a testament to the eternal and unchanging nature of God's will. It serves as anchor of steadfastness of divine purpose. There is assurance in enduring principles set forth by God, the Creator of Heaven and Earth.

Guiding Light for Living

God's word is a manual for life; a guide that leads through the intricates of existence. What could be more worthy of pursuit than understanding the revelations of an all-knowing God? Drawing near to God who intimately knows everyone best is a compelling desire. Doing so, allows His word takes residence in people hearts.

God imparts hearts by dropping His word into heart through the power of Holy Spirit and the timeless God's word in the Bible. Ezra 7:6, " This Ezra went up from Babylon; and he was a ready scribe in the law of Moses, which the Lord God of Israel had given: and the king granted him all his request, according to the hand of the Lord his God upon him." "For Ezra had devoted himself to the study and observance of the Law of the Lord and to teaching its decrees and laws in Israel" (Ezra 7:10)

When believers immerse themselves in God's word, a transformative journey begins. God shapes the thoughts, directs, steps, and breathes of His children through His word and revelation. In a world saturated with human opinions, distinction between truth and falsehood becomes clearer when grounded in God's word. Amidst the clamor of worldly propositions, there lies a profound truth that only God possesses the power of enduring truth. Having created the world and everything within it, His perspective remains supreme.

The unwavering promise of God as revealed in Revelation 3:8 which says, "For the promises of God are 'Yes' and 'Amen." Embracing the profound assurance embedded in God's word is utmost important. For therein lies the path to a deeper relationship with Jesus as a continuous journey that transcends the fading distractions of the world. It's important to prioritize the genuine words of the Almighty God above all other words. For in God's word is everlasting truth. Understanding God's word is a subject that has captivated the minds and hearts of many for centuries. Although, ways in which individuals perceive and interpret these divine God's word are diverse among various religions, traditions, and personal experiences.

Nourished by the Word

In the profound words of Jeremiah 15:16 (KJV) resonates through the ages: "Thy words were found, and I did eat them; and thy word was unto me the joy and rejoicing of my heart: for I am called by thy name, O LORD God of hosts." This verse beautifully captures the essence of finding nourishment and joy in the divine words of God. Psalms 1:2 (KJV) further amplifies the reward of immersing lives in God's word: "But his delight is in the law of the LORD, and in his law doth he meditates day and night." This confirms the intimate connection God wants to connect with those who believe and trust in God's word. It is a level of intimacy with God when believers continuously meditate on the words of the Almighty God in truth.

The Book of James, emphases on the wisdom of God and urges believers to move beyond passive listening, but become active doers of the Word. The verse warns against self-deception, emphasizing the transformative power of sincerely application of the Word of God. The richness of God's words encompasses a vast spectrum of wisdom, teachings, and admonishments. Believers are called not only to hear but to let the words of Christ dwell in them continually. There is a wellspring of guidance, wisdom, and deepening connection with God Almighty and continuous dwelling in God's word. James 1: 22-25 says, "But be ye doers of the word, and not hearers only, deceiving your own selves. For if any be a hearer of the word, and not a doer, he is like unto a man beholding his natural face in a glass: For he beholdeth himself, and goeth his way, and straightway forgetteth what manner of man he was. But whoso looketh into the perfect law of liberty, and continueth therein, he being not a forgetful hearer, but a doer of the work, this man shall be blessed in his deed."

Prayer and Meditation

Personal communication with God through prayer and meditation is important in relationship to God Almighty. In these moments of stillness, individuals may receive guidance, inspiration, or God's presence. May we like the psalmist, and the prophet Jeremiah find joy and delight in the timeless power and wisdom in the words of God.

Chapter 6: Impacts in God's Word

Truthful and Fruit Words

Humans are God's workmanship, crafted in Christ Jesus for good works. The words of God serve as the guiding force that propels human beings towards fulfilling God's good pleasure. It is through the declaration of what has been seen and heard from God the Father, Son and Holy Spirit that divine promises manifest. Crucial to the effectiveness of God's words is the infusion of faith as highlighted in Hebrews 4:2 (KJV), "For unto us was the gospel preached, as well as unto them: but the word preached did not profit them, not being mixed with faith in them that heard it."

Faith in God underscores the symbiotic relationship between the words of God and the faith of the hearers. When faith and words of God are harmoniously intertwine there accentuating and transformative power of God. God's word is a profound testament to the creative power of God's words found in the assertion that through faith the world was framed by the Word of God. This powerful reality reiterates the impact of God's word, reinforcing the creative power in God's word. God's word manifest through harmonious interplay of God's words and the receptive faith in the word.

God's Word in Fulfillment

God's words reaffirm the certainty of profound confirmation and verification of God's mandates. The word of the Almighty God are not mere echoes lost in the void but promises destined to be fulfilled. Within the words of God lie the very pillars of wisdom, instruction, and understanding. Nathan was guided by the divine vision spoke to Samuel in alignment with the words of God. The events bore witness to the undeniable truth embedded in words of God. The power of God's word extends beyond prophets; believers themselves become conduits through which His words manifest.

"For I am the LORD: I will speak, and the word that I shall speak shall come to pass; it shall be no more prolonged: for in your days, O rebellious house, will I say the word, and will perform it, saith the Lord GOD" (Ezekiel 12:25 KJV). These words serve as a testament to the unwavering commitment of God to bring His divine plan to fruition. God's words are not mere rhetoric; they are a blazing fire within the hearts of the faithful, a force, so potent that it cannot be contained.

Life and eternity are woven into the fabric of God's words and those who have experienced the transformative power of God's word can testify to the indomitable strength through God's words. Within the pages of the Bible, is confirmed the words of God endure eternally. The stories of Joseph and the instructions given to the Apostle Paul stand as enduring proof of the divine promises finding fulfillment in the course of human history.

Joseph's life serves as a testament to the transformative power and purpose from God's words. Sold into slavery, imprisoned, yet ultimately becoming a Prime Minister. Joseph's unwavering sense of direction enabled him to endure the most challenging circumstances with faith and resilience. Despite being betrayed by his brothers, sold into slavery, falsely accused, and imprisoned, Joseph remained steadfast in his trust in God's plan. His ability to see beyond his immediate hardships and maintain his faith allowed him to navigate the trials he faced with remarkable strength and purpose.

His declaration in Genesis 50:20 reveals a profound understanding of divine providence and the bigger picture of God's purpose. When Joseph says, "But as for you, ye thought evil against me; but God meant it unto good," he recognizes that while others intended harm for him, God used those very actions to bring about a greater good. This statement reflects Joseph's deep insight into the nature of God's sovereignty, demonstrating that even the most painful experiences can be woven into a larger plan for good. Joseph's perspective teaches that faith in God's purpose can transform suffering into a testimony of hope, resilience, and redemption.

Impact of God's Word

"Make haste and get thee quickly out of Jerusalem: for they will not receive thy testimony concerning me." God with omniscient knowledge discerns the hearts that will embrace His words and those that will resist. The unfolding story of Joseph's life and the journey of Apostle Paul serve as living testaments to the undeniable reliability of God's words.

In the grand tapestry of existence, the promises made by the Almighty is transcending, leaving indelible marks on human experience. Apostle Paul urges Timothy with profound wisdom: "Take heed to yourself and to the doctrine. Continue in them, for in doing this, you will save both yourself and those who hear you." This command explains the essence of a fulfilling and purposeful life. Believers are admonished to explore the significance of heeding to words of God and the transformative power it holds for humanity.

The admonition to "take heed" serves as a compass for personal introspection and spiritual growth. By embracing guidance in God's word, believers are encouraged to examine their actions, thoughts, and beliefs in the light of God's words. This self-awareness becomes a vehicle for positive change, fostering deeper connection with God.

The directive to "continue in them" emphasizes the importance of steadfastness in upholding the principles of sound doctrine. The journey of faith is not a one-time event but a continuous commitment to living according to God's word. This persistence contributes not only to personal salvation but also sets an example for others, creating positive effect of righteous standing and love for others.

The promise of salvation, both for oneself and those who hear the message, underscores the transformative impact of aligning one's life with divine principles of God.

As believers walk in the light of God's word, they become beacons of hope and inspiration for others. The effect extends beyond personal salvation to the salvation of those who are touched by the testimony and righteous living of the faithful.

The call to "take heed to yourself and to the doctrine" is an invitation to a life of purpose, self-reflection, and continuous growth in the principles of faith. By embracing the Words of God, individuals are not only securing their own salvation but also becoming instruments of salvation for those who are touched by their lives. It is a profound journey of living according to God's word for the betterment of oneself and the world.

Embracing God's Words

In a world filled with uncertainties, believers find solace and strength in the timeless wisdom from God's words. The unchanging God's word assures believers that word of God will inevitably come to pass. This is profound assurance exemplified in God's word with Moses. God's plans and purposes for mankind align with God existence always stand forever, resolute to circumstances, and un-annullable.

God's words serve as a wellspring of refuge and strength, providing unwavering support to those who seek solace in God's word. God divine promises are swiftly released as a present help. As a beacon of hope in the midst of tribulations. Word of God as a source of encouragement stems from its unwavering reliability. The Gospel of Christ, described as the power of God unto salvation confirms the transformative impact of divine words of God across cultural and geographical boundaries.

In times when reality appears contrary to the promises of God, believers are encouraged to stand firm in faith. Demonstrating faith is a steadfast conviction expresses with boldness becomes a powerful testimony of divine power amidst challenges. Even as the world around undergoes changes, believers are reminded not to succumb to fear, drawing strength from the assurance that, "though the earth be removed, and though the mountains be carried into the midst of the sea," God's promises remain unshakable.

Words of God comforts, offering divine perspective that transcends the temporal challenges of life. This steadfast faith becomes a testament to the enduring power of God's word, shaping not only lives but also becoming a source of encouragement for journey of faith.

For His Name Sake

For His Name's Sake" holds profound significance in the Bible. Particularly in relation to Jesus Christ. This affirms God actions in fulfilling His promises is for the sake of His own name which is synonymous with His character, glory, and reputation. "For His Name's Sake" also points to the manifestation of God's glory. God's acts, whether in creation, redemption, or judgment are designed to display God's glory and majesty. Through the redemptive work of Jesus Christ, God's glory is revealed in salvation of souls, demonstrating His mercy and grace for "His Name Sake."

The concept is deeply rooted in the bible revealing the divine nature of God and the redemptive mission of Jesus Christ.

"For His Name's Sake" carries the divine purpose, authority, and redemptive plan of God as revealed through Jesus Christ. It is a powerful reminder of God's faithfulness, sovereignty, and the ultimate fulfillment of His promises for the sake of His glorious name. Believers are often called to live lives "for His Name's Sake." This means that their actions, conduct, and testimonies should reflect the character and love of God. By doing so, they become ambassadors of His name, bearing witness to the transformative power through relationship with Jesus Christ.

In the New Testament, the ultimate expression of "For His Name's Sake" is revealed through the mission of Jesus Christ. The salvation of humanity achieved through Jesus' sacrificial death and resurrection is not only an act of love but also a demonstration of God's righteousness and faithfulness to His name. The Apostle Paul emphasized this in his letters attributing the salvation of believers to God's grace and the glory of His Name.

Essence of Truth

God's words are timeless powerful and true at all seasons. Oracle of the LORD explains profound reality that God's Words are not just utterances but the very essence of truth and creation. God's word explores the omnipotent power inherent in God's word, tracing its effectiveness from the Genesis of existence to the eternity. This paragraph unfolds the resonance of profound words of God. Inspiration from the Scripture: "In the beginning was the Word, and the Word was with God, and the Word was God." God's words have transformative power, a power that breathes life into every aspect of creation.

There is deep connection between God the Creator and His creation. God is bound to mankind by the breath of God infused within every created entity. God's words are not fleeting, are powerful and enduring through eternity. "Heaven and earth shall pass away, but my words shall not pass away, shows the enduring legacy of divine truth that transcends the world. In a world marked by trends and constant changes, God's word remains unchanging.

While the world evolves, God's truth remains unwavering and steadfast. God's word is perfect and requires no correction or improvement. God's word stands as a testament to the enduring nature of truth, shaping the very foundation of existence since the beginning of time. In a world filled with uncertainties, this literary journey becomes a source of solace and enlightenment, reaffirming the timeless God's words. The enduring truth in the words of God has been persisted since creation and will continue.

Perfect words of God are profound and unchanging truth that endures till kingdom come. Take for instance, Jeremiah 30:18 "which says '" With resounding authority, declares to the ancient city of Jerusalem, 'Thou shalt be inhabited,' and to the venerable cities of Judah, 'Ye shall be rebuilt, and I will elevate the dilapidated places to their former glory." This verse is a beacon of hope, echoed through the ages, assuring the resurgence of life and prosperity.

All God's words are inspirational. Words of God are not merely for the restoration of physical structures but more profoundly for the spiritual. God's people are vessels of worship and testimonies to the enduring faithfulness of the Almighty God. The Creator in His infinite wisdom ordained His promises to unfold not merely for the sake of the city's inhabitants but for the manifestation of His own glory and praises that shall never be silenced.

Oracle of the LORD understands that uncertainties abound; however, God's word serves as a source of solace and enlightenment and reaffirming the timeless God's words and commandments. Recognizing God's truth that has endures since the creation and continue till kingdom come.

Chapter 7: Reassurance of God's Word

God's Words Are True and Powerful

God's words are powerful and enduring forever. "Heaven and earth shall pass away, but my words shall not pass away," is a reminder of the enduring legacy of divine truth. The truth remains forever. The world trends change from time to time but what God says never change. God's word needs no correction and improvement. It stays forever. God's word remains the same from the beginning of time. Oracle of the LORD stands as a testament to the enduring words of God. Through the ages and existence of creature words of God remain same. Words of God are not mere utterances but the very essence of truth and creation. From the Genesis to the timeless veracity, word of God unfolds profound endurance.

"In the beginning was the Word and the Word was with God and the Word was God," expresses the enduring power inherent in the word of God. God breathes life into every aspect of creation. God the creator and His creations are deeply connected because of the breath of God.

Oracle of the LORD inspire readers to reflect on divine assurance as confirmed in Psalm 148:5. "Let them praise the name of the Lord: for he commanded and they were created." In the face of life's uncertainties, drawing inspiration from the omnipotent Words of God is paramount. Recognizing therein lies power that surpasses all human understanding; power that molds the very foundations of existence.

The assurance embedded in the Words of God are confirm throughout the world by believers, unyielding force that precisely achieves effectiveness of God's word. There is source of unwavering confidence and confidence in God's word that transcends limitations of mortal word.

Divine Utterance

In a world where uncertainties abound, God's word serves as a source of solace and enlightenment, reaffirming the timeless power of God's words. God's truth that has endured since the creation and continue till kingdom come. Psalm 148:5, unequivocally resonates through the ages: "Let them praise the name of the LORD for he commanded, and they were made." This verse captures the very essence of God's word. God's word is a word that possesses the unparalleled ability to bring creation into existence.

Words of God stand as a testament to the unwavering assurance of powerful words of God. Unlike the words of human which are subject to some constraints or limitations. People's word can change by unpredictable human emotion or unforeseen circumstances and individual abilities. God's word is divine, resolute, and steadfast. The word that carries within the potency to manifest exact declaration.

God's Word is not mere rhetoric; it is the omnipotent force that breathes life into existence. When God speaks, creation responds. This divine assurance extends beyond the mere articulation of His will. God's word is a decree that shapes the very framework of reality.

In contrast between God's word and other sources of words; God's word is real and stands as it is. Human words are susceptible to the frailties inherent in nature. People expressions may be color by limitations which may be hindered by uncertainties and emotions.

The Scripture

Scriptures are Christian manual and references. This is why the Scriptures take form of Doctrine, Belief, Reproof, Disapprove, Correction, Inoculate, Amendment, Righteousness, knowledge, and information.

1. **Doctrine** refers to a set of beliefs or teachings that are held and promoted by Christians. In God's words, doctrine encompasses the principles and teachings derived from God's word, which guide the faith and practices of believers.

2. **Belief** is the acceptance of God's word as the truth. Belief is faith in doctrines and teachings of God's word. Is rust in God and adherence to the truths.

3. **Reproof** means expressing disapproval or criticism of someone's behavior or actions. In God's words, reproof often refers to the act of admonishing or correction when astray from the path of righteousness.

4. **Disapprove** is to disapprove means to have an unfavorable opinion about something. In Christianity disapproval refers to God's judgment against actions or behaviors that are contrary to God's commands and teachings.

5. **Correction** is the action of rectifying or improving something that is wrong or inaccurate. Within the framework of Christian teachings, correction involves guiding believers back to the correct path of behavior and faith in line with God's will.

6. **Inoculate** mean to protect someone from harmful influences. This could involve teaching and instilling spiritual truths that protect believers from moral and spiritual corruption.

7. **Amendment** refers to the process of making changes or improvements. In Christianity, it involves adjusting actions or beliefs to align with God's words and principles.

8. **Righteousness** is the quality of being morally right or justifiable. Righteousness is living in accordance with God's laws and commandments, demonstrating virtues such as integrity, honesty, and piety.

9. **Knowledge** refers to understanding and awareness of facts, information, and gifts. knowledge often pertains to a deep understanding of God's truthful words, commands, and the influence of the Holy Spirit.

10. **Information** is data or facts provided or learned about God. In Christianity, information are words of God, words from God, scripture and revelations.

11. **Morally Correct and Justifiable** means actions or beliefs that are ethically sound and can be defended based on moral principles. Morally Correct and Justifiable are behaviors and decisions that are in harmony with God's words and commandments upheld as right and just according to Godly principles.

Understanding these terms, lead to better application of Godly teachings of faith, values, and Godly principles. Principle. Scripture messages are direct communications and revelations from God.

Unwavering Word of God

Another aspect of profound word of God is unwavering true relationship that exit between God, the Holy Spirit, and the Son, Jesus Christ. In exploring the dynamic interplay of the Father, the Holy Spirit, and Jesus Christ, there is a harmonious triune, each distinct, yet inseparable, working in concert to reveal the multifaceted nature of God.

God, in His infinite wisdom communicates with humanity in various ways. It is the same Spirit, the same God, yet with different modes of ministration. This divine diversity in communication reflects the richness of how the Creator's engages with His creation. The Holy Trinity unfolds, revealing facets of the divine nature that resonate uniquely with the human experience.

Amidst of God the father, Son, and The Holy Spirit, one unassailable truth prevails. The assurance that the words of God are final. The LORD in His sovereignty always stands behind His words. This unwavering commitment is beautifully described in Mark 16:17.

Mark 16:17, "And these signs shall follow them that believe; In my name shall they cast out devils; they shall speak with new tongues." This statement serves as a testament to the potency of the divine word of God. It affirms that those who believe in the name of the Lord are endowed with the authority to speak and witness miracles. This authority stems not from human prowess but is a direct consequence of the unshakable assurance that underlies God's word.

As journey through revelations within the pages of Oracle of the LORD, may you find solace in the unchanging God's promises. May you be enveloped in the profound assurance that the words of God are not fleeting or conditional but stand as eternal and irrevocable truths.

Reflection on John 1:1-4

Gospel of John, chapter 1:1-4 reveals the essence of God's Word. The scripture states, "In the beginning was the Word, and the Word was with God, and the Word was God. The same was in the beginning with God. All things were made by him; and without him was not anything made that was made. In him was life, and the life was the light of men" (John 1:1-4). This foundational passage expresses the divine power in God's word, highlighting its role in creation and its embodiment of life and light. Understanding the significance of God's word becomes crucial in Christian journey of faith.

The scripture is not merely an intellectual exercise but a spiritual discipline that fosters a deep connection with God. The Bible encourages us to meditate on God's word. This meditation serves as a calm and peaceful space, to commune with God in a meaningful way.

Meditation goes beyond simply reading the scripture, it involves carving out dedicated time to be alone with God. Establishing a regular routine for meditation provides a framework to connect with the LORD. Whether in the morning, evening, or any other convenient time, creating quite space allows personal relationship with God.

During quite time, believers acknowledge God's presence, express gratitude for His love, grace, and faithfulness. Intimate interaction is based on the assurance that God is faithful to forgive, as mentioned in 1 John 1:9. It is a time to bring requests and concerns before God trusting that God cares for His people.

Meditating on God's word is an invitation to a transformative journey. It is through this focused connection that believers experience the life and light described in John 1:1-4. By meditating on richness of God's words, believers encounter the living Word that shape lives, illuminate paths, and connect in deeper relationship with the Creator.

The importance of God's Word lies not only in its historical and theological significance but also in its practical application in daily lives. By engaging in the discipline of meditation on God's word, then openness to the transformative power that leads to a more profound understanding and a closer walk with the Creator.

Intimacy Through Meditation

The importance of God's word and transformative power cannot be overlooked. It is embedded in the practice of reading, listening, and being open to God's voice. This profound engagement is not a one-way communication rather, a dynamic interplay that involves both hearing and responding to God's guidance.

Reading and listening to God's voice and being open to his guidance is a pivotal aspect of Christianity. This involves keen sensitivity to the Holy Spirit, allowing His presence to direct prayers and meditation on God's Word. Doing so, opens deeper understanding of God's will. In the space of meditation, prayer takes on a new dimension it becomes a two-way conversation.

Interactive prayer creates deeper intimacy with God. Which fosters profound connection that goes beyond words. Psalm 148:5 beautifully captures the authority of God's word in the act of creation: "Let every created thing give praise to the LORD, for he issued his command, and they came into being." This verse in psalm emphasizes the power of God's voice, illustrating that His command brings forth existence.

As believers meditate on God's Word and engage in this divine dialogue, they participate in the ongoing creation with God. The same power that spoke the universe into existence is at work in prayers, shaping and molding lives according to God's purposes. The practice of reading, listening, and being open to God's voice is not just a religious routine; is an invitation to a transformative experience.

Through meditation on God's Word and active engagement in two-way prayer, deeper intimacy with god is unlocked and to a greater understanding of God's purposes. Is discovered. Let praise the name of the Lord, recognizing His command as the creative force that brings forth human existence. For he said, "Let them praise the name of the Lord: for he commanded, and they were created" (Psalm 148:5) This verse is a powerful reminder of the relationship between God and His creation. God's word brought life and called to respond with praise. It reflects a cycle of divine action. God commands creation existence and then creation praises its Creator. This points to the ultimate sovereignty of God and the purpose of all creation is to glorify and honor God. This emphasizes the power of God's word in creation and calls all of creation to worship Him.

The call to *"praise the name of the Lord"* is an instruction not just for humans but for all creation. The

Psalm calls on everything that exists; angels, the sun, moon, stars, animals, and even inanimate objects like mountains and seas to praise God. Everything that exists reflects God's glory and therefore is called to honor and worship Him. This act of praise is not based on choice but on the fact that all things owe exitance to God's creative word. Creation itself glorifies God simply by existing and fulfilling its intended purpose. The name of the Lord is more than just a label. It represents God's character, authority, and essence. To *"praise the name of the Lord"* is to acknowledge God's greatness, holiness, and sovereignty over all things. When creation praises the name of the Lord, they acknowledge both the creative power and the sustaining presence of God

Fruitfulness in God's Word

Fruitfulness in understanding and living out God's word comes from the Holy Spirit. The Spirit enlightens and helps people to live by truths. In Ephesians 1:17-18: Paul prays for the Spirit of wisdom and revelation for believers to know God better. 1 Corinthians 2:10-14: The Spirit reveals deep truths of God that man cannot understand.

Insufficiency of Human Effort

Relying solely on human wisdom or effort (the flesh) leads to limited understanding and spiritual stagnation. The flesh in its natural state cannot produce spiritual fruit. "The flesh profited nothing", "flesh" represents human efforts and understanding without divine intervention. Which underscores that mere human effort or literal interpretation without spiritual insight is of no value in manifesting God's will. Romans 8:6-8: emphasizes that mind governed by flesh is death, but the mind governed by the Holy Spirit is life and peace. "For to be carnally minded is death; but to be spiritually minded is life and peace. Because the carnal mind is enmity against God: for it is not subject to the law of God, neither indeed can be. So, then they that are in the flesh cannot please God."

Life-Giving Power of Jesus' Words

God's words are life-giving because they are empowered by the Holy Spirit. As people internalize and obey God's word, they experience spiritual growth and fruitfulness. John 15:7-8, Abiding in Jesus and His words leads to bearing much fruit. "If ye abide in me, and my words abide in you, ye shall ask what ye will, and it shall be done unto you. Herein is my Father glorified, that ye bear much fruit; so, shall ye be my disciples."

Practical Application for Believers

1.   **Dependence on the Holy Spirit:** Cultivating deep reliance on the Holy Spirit for understanding and applying God's word honestly. This involves regular prayer, seeking Holy Spirit's guidance, and being open to His leading. John 14:26: The Holy Spirit teaches and reminds believers the words."

2.   **Engaging with God's Word:** Regularly reading and meditating on word makes God's words become alive and effective. Joshua 1:8: Meditate on the Word Day and night for divine success and prosperity. God categorizes success differently from the world version of success.

3. **Transformation through Obedience:** Apply the teachings of Jesus to daily life, allowing transformation thoughts, attitudes, and actions. This is how fruitfulness manifests. James 1:22: "Be doers of the word, not hearers only."

Community and Growth: Engaging in community services encourages growth. Holy Spirit works through communal study and worship. Hebrews 10:24-25: incite one another toward love and good deeds. It says "And let us consider one another to provoke unto love and to good works: Not forsaking the assembling of brethren as the manner of some, but exhorting one another and so much the more, as ye see the day approaching"

John 6:63 emphasizes the crucial role of the Holy Spirit in bringing spiritual life and understanding through God's words. "It is the spirit that quickeneth; the flesh profiteth nothing: the words that I speak unto you, they are spirit, and they are life". Human effort alone is insufficient. It is the Holy Spirit that quickens, bringing true fruitfulness. Believers are called to rely on the Holy Spirit, immerse themselves in God's word and live out these truths, resulting in a life that bears abundant spiritual fruit.

Chapter 8: A Biblical Exploration

Ways God Communicates

In the beginning was the Word, and the Word was with God and the Word was God. (John 1:1) These profound words set the foundation for understanding the sovereign power embedded in God's Word. All through ages, "In the beginning" emphasizes the timeless existence of the Word. John 1:1 confirmed Divine sovereign of God's words which transcend temporal boundaries.

Exploring Revelation 3:8, "I know your works. Behold, I have set before you an open door which no one is able to shut." This testifies to the witness of the sovereign power of God's words. God's words manifest as unassailable and open-door to revelation beyond human comprehension. "Let them praise the name of the LORD for he commanded, and they were created." (Psalm 148:5) testify the creative authority inherent in God's words confirming the accurate words of God that brings forth existence. Psalm 30:12 "As the shadows of adversity yielded to the dawn of deliverance, a refrain of gratitude rises from the depths of the soul. To the end that my glory may sing praise to thee and not be silent" This was declared by the psalmist as exultant testament to the transformative power of God word.

Potent Words of God

Many believers find rest in words of God. "I will give thanks unto thee forever." The permanence of gratitude for God's mercy and goodness. Jeremiah 30:18, "He declared to the ancient city of Jerusalem, thou shalt be inhabited and to the venerable cities of Judah, Ye shall be rebuilt, and I will elevate the dilapidated places to their former glory." This verse is a beacon of hope through the ages, assuring the resurgence of life and prosperity in the once desolate places. God's word rectorates with structures and profound for revival. Through words of God, a person becomes a vessel of worship and testimonies to the enduring faithfulness of the Almighty God. The Creator in His infinite wisdom has ordained this promise not merely for the sake of the city's inhabitants but for the manifestation of His own glory.

God's Word in Action

Drawing parallels between God's Word and captivating performance agree with God's word is important. Word of God unfolds through acts of providence, miracles, and the orchestration of events that align with the promises in the words.

Behind the Utterance

Contrary to other sources of voices, God's word underscores the intimate involvement of God in His creation. His Word is not a distant copy but a deliberate and purposeful expression that surely manifest.

Shepherd's Voice

Drawing from Jesus statement in John 10:27, "My sheep hear my voice, and I know them, and they follow me," This verse confirmed the importance of recognizing and heeding the voice of the Shepherd. God's words serve as a lifeline connection to God. God's voice transcends the mundane and bridges the gap between human heart and the world.

Prophetic Voice

Throughout history, people have reported receiving divine messages through visions and dreams. Prophets and seers often receive insights into the divine will through these experiences. "Prophetic Utterances of God" highlight the special relationship between God and His chosen messengers. Words proclaimed by prophets are seen as directly inspired and entrusted by the God.

Prophetic Utterances

Amos 3:7-8 resonate with the weight of divine authority and revelation. It serves as a beacon illuminating the relationship between God and His prophets. The timeless imperative of prophecy. "Surely the Lord GOD will do nothing, but He revealed his secret unto his servants the prophets." God in His infinite wisdom chooses to disclose His divine intentions to His faithful servants from time to time. God's words are foundational truth. Secrets or divine disclosure which is partnership between the Creator and His chosen vessels. Prophets play indispensable role of God's divine plan for humanity. God can establish intimacy and trust with His trusted vessels.

God confides in His appointed messengers sharing insights reserved for those who walk closely with Him. It's proof to profound connection between God and human. Amos 3:7 "The lion hath roared, who will not fear? The Lord GOD hath spoken, who can but prophesy?" Roaring lion serves as a metaphor for the thunderous voice of God. It reverberates across the landscape of human consciousness, evoking awe reverence and healthy fear of the God's Voice. Fear is not merely natural response, but acknowledgment of the overwhelming power and authority inherent in God's word.

The question posed, "who can but prophesy?" refers to compulsion that grips the prophet in the wake of divine revelation. This is not a matter of choice but an undeniable call to action and a stirring within the depths of the soul that impels one to speak forth the words of God. Is difficult to withhold such revelation.

The above verses capture relationship between God and human-beings where God's sovereign intersect with human agenda through the conduit of prophecy. This is a reminder that the prophetic voice isn't merely a relic of ancient times but a living reality. Jeremiah 1:9 (NIV) "Then the Lord reached out his hand and touched my mouth and said to me, 'I have put my words in your mouth." The book of Jeremiah provides a profound insight into the prophetic calling and the relationship between God and His chosen messengers. The verse illustrates a powerful encounter between prophet Jeremiah and the divine presence.

The Lord reaching out and touching Jeremiah's mouth symbolizes the divine commissioning of the prophet. It signifies a direct and intimate connection between human as God messengers and Godly sources of the message. The act of touching the mouth is symbolic of God appointing and enabling Jeremiah to speak on His behalf. "I have put my words in your mouth," confirmed the essence of prophetic utterances. The authority and content of the message are not generated by the prophet's own thoughts or intentions but are divinely bestowed. The prophet becomes a vessel through which God communicates His will, guidance, and sometimes warnings to the people.

These verses emphasize the absolute trust God placed upon His prophets. It proved the divine origin and authority of God's word. The prophetic role involves faithfully conveying the messages given by God even when the message may be challenging or unpopular. Throughout Christianity, prophets are seen as intermediaries between God and people. Prophets are channels through which God communicates His plans, desires, and instructions to His people. The obedience and faithfulness of prophets in delivering God's messages are crucial components of their role.

Believer Role

As believers in this performance, it is important for believers to reflect on their role in alignment with words of God. Through faith, obedience, and a receptive heart, human become conduits through which God's Word manifests, playing a part in promises of God. Reflecting on constant words of God, enables believers to gain a comprehensive understanding of God's will for His people.

This multifaceted exploration enhances the appreciation for the richness and depth of God's words as active, not a static but dynamic force, eagerly performing in the intricacies of God's acts. There is solace, inspiration, and renewal sense of purpose in participating and performance in God's promises.

Chapter 9: God is My Pasture

God is my Shepherd.

In demonstration of faith, God's words emerge as both a comforting balm and a protective shield, guiding humanity along the intricate path of life. God establishes profound connections between Him and His children, drawing inspiration from the bible and seeing God as the Shepherd, tenderly caring for His flock through the power of His words. As a shepherd, God demonstrates the Comforting and Protective role through His word.

God's Shepherds confirm the nurturing and protective attributes of God through God's own words. God establishes an intimate connection with humans, assuming the role of a loving caretaker who tends to his children needs, protects them from harm and guides them to green pastures.

Comforting God's Words

God's words are sources of solace and reassurance. When believers akin to gentle whisper of God's word in the depths of their soul and heart, that settles it. The comforting aspect of God's word provides anchor for believers, offering peace amidst life's storms. Psalm 23:1, "The Lord is my shepherd; I shall not want." God is My pasture living and powerful shepherd as the Psalmist says.

Psalm 30:12 speaks about overcoming hard times and celebrating God's help. It says, "So that my heart will sing your praises and not be silent, O Lord my God, I will give you thanks forever." This verse is a reminder that in midst of life's challenges remain grateful to God's and trust in God's word that can never fail. Even in tough times, God can still be trusted. He will surely bring His words to pass. This is an inspiration to always thank God for His unwavering promises. Believers find refuge in embracing God's presence, a guardian whose words offer not just comfort, but a promise of enduring protection.

Protective shield

In the journey of life, words of God stand as a comforting and protective shield, sense of security and solace. In moments of uncertainty, word of God serves as guiding light, offering reassurance and sanctuary to those who trust in God's words.

Hope Amidst Chaos

The profound wisdom embedded in God's word unfolds like a gentle embrace, cradling believers in warmth of God's unfailing love. Throughout the Holy Bible verses believer find solace in the face of adversity, strength in times of weakness, and hope when shadows loom large. Each word resonates with a promise as a reminder of assurance that God is always with His people.

In life's challenges, words of God become a melody that soothes the heart and uplifts the spirit. Through the existence, whispering courage in the face of fear and serenity amidst chaos. Like a protective cloak, words of God shield believers from despair and infuse them with senses of purpose. The comforting tone of God's word transcend the boundaries of human word. It is a source of solace, a beacon of hope that stands unwavering in the tempest of life. The scripture encourages God's people to immerse themselves in words of God. In times of doubt, God's word become fortress and a refuge for the weary heart. Embracing God's comforting words serve as source of strength. Believers find strength in surrendering and peace in certainty of true and enduring words of God.

Potent Word of God

God's word is a timeless truth and relevant to all situations at all seasons. In the scriptures, people find affirmation of the power and truth embedded in the words of God. Psalm 33:4 KJV declares, "For the word of the LORD is right; And all his works are done in truth." This foundational truth establishes the correctness and integrity of God's word making it relevant and active in every situation and across all eras of time. The Righteousness of God's Word in Psalm 33:4 serves as a beacon guiding believers to recognize the inherent righteousness through the word and Christ the expression of God's words. It is not subject to error or falsehood rather it stands as an unwavering standard of truth inspiring good works.

The unfailing accomplishment according to Isaiah 55:11 KJV unveils the dynamic nature of God's word, "so shall my word be that goeth forth out of my mouth: it shall not return unto me void, but it shall accomplish that which

I please and it shall prosper in the thing whereto I sent it." This is assurance that God's word is never empty or in vain. It unfailingly accomplishes God's purposes, bringing fulfillment in alignment with God's will.

Word of God is always directed towards God's Glory probing deeper into Isaiah 55:11, reveal effectiveness of God's word when directed towards the glory of God. The word of God is not just a tool for personal gain but a divine force that achieves its highest potential when aligned with reasons to glorify God Almighty.

The Oracle of the LORD Book reaffirmed Psalm 33:4 and Isaiah 55:11, the timeless truth that the word of the LORD is not only right and truthful but also actively effective in accomplishing God's divine purposes. This revelation is a call to align lives with the divine direction confined in the word of God. Recognizing unfailing potency and ultimate purpose of bringing glory to God.

Divine Utterances

God's words act is a shield, providing protection and guidance to those who earnestly seek His presence. The psalmist declares in Psalm 119:105, "Your word is a lamp to my feet and a light to my path." This illustrates God's word as shield to humanity, can protect from stumbling in the life's uncertainties.

Navigating Journey

In life, believers find guidance and direction through the unwavering promises and teachings found in God's words. The Scriptures become a roadmap, offering insights, wisdom, and divine counsel that navigate the complexities of existence, ensuring that the faithful traverse the journey of life with purpose and divine assurance. In the journey of faith, believers are encouraged to marvel at the enduring legacy in God's words. Throughout history, God's words serves as both a compass and a map guiding people through life's intricate terrain. It offers solace in the unchanging God's promises, serving as a wellspring of strength, purpose, and everlasting joy.

Cultivating the Connection

As stewards of God, God divinely connect to His children and encourages to cultivate attuned spirit, receptive to the Shepherd's voice amidst the noise of the world. Through prayer, meditation, and deep engagement with the Scriptures fostering profound communion with God. The comforting and protective role of God's words is an integral aspect of Christianity. As believers embrace God as the Shepherd and acknowledge the transformative power of God's truths, they find themselves securely guided, comforted, and protected along the winding paths of life. May you continue to listen to the Shepherd's voice and draw strength and assurance from the eternal promises in God's word.

Chapter 10: Comfort Reassuring

Transformative Powerful Word

The Word of God is living, quick, sharp, and powerful and holds unparalleled significance. It a lively oracle given to humanity, possessing the ability to pierce into the deepest soul and spirit. This profound impact on lives emphasizes that the Word of God is not merely a collection of teachings but dynamic force that interacts with and transforms lives. By engaging deeply with the Word, people can experience growth, moral clarity, and closer relationship with God. The statement, "The Word of God possesses the ability to pierce into the deepest soul and spirit," underscores its powerful and transformative nature.

Key Attributes

Hebrews 4:12 (NIV), says: "For the word of God is alive and active. Sharper than any double-edged sword, it penetrates even to dividing soul and spirit, joints and marrow; it judges the thoughts and attitudes of the heart."

This verse highlights several key attributes of the Word of God:

1. **Alive and Active:** Unlike ordinary texts, the Word of God is living and dynamic, capable of interacting with the reader on a profound level.

2.   **Sharper than a Double-Edged Sword:** Words of God is defined and able to penetrates. Just as a sword can cut through physical matter, the Word of God can cut through spiritual and moral layers.

3.   **Penetrating:** It can reach the deepest parts of a person, beyond superficial understanding or surface-level behavior.

4.   **Judges Thoughts and Attitudes:** It discerns and evaluates the innermost thoughts and intentions, providing clarity and truth about one's spiritual state.

5.   **Transformation:** The piercing nature of the Word of God signifies its power to transform lives. It can convict, guide, and inspire changes in people lives.

6.   **Discernment:** It provides wisdom and insight that is able to discern truth from falsehood and right from wrong. This discernment extends to understanding oneself better, recognizing one's own faults and strengths.

7.   **Healing and Wholeness:** Just as a surgeon's scalpel can bring about healing by cutting away diseased tissue, the Word of God can bring healing by addressing and removing sin and spiritual ailments.

Practical Implications

1. **Personal Reflection and Growth:** Engaging with the Word of God encourages deep personal reflection. It a challenge to examine lives, thoughts, and motives in light of God's word.

2. **Moral and Ethical Guidance:** It serves as a moral compass, offering guidance on how to live a righteous and fulfilling life. Its teachings shape ethical behavior and decision-making.

3. **Comfort and Encouragement:** In times of distress or uncertainty, the Word of God provides comfort and encouragement, reminding believers of God's promises and presence.

4. **Community and Teaching:** The Word of God is central to teaching, preaching, and communal worship. It unifies believers and directs communal values and actions.

5. **Intimacy with God:** By engaging deeply with the Word, people can experience a more intimate relationship with God. Deep penetration of words of God into the soul and spirit fosters a closer connection and understanding of God's character and purposes.

Living Word

Jeremiah, a prophet of the Old Testament, vividly expressed the life-giving quality of the Word of God. Jeremiah expressed finding words of God and eating it. This illustrates how the Word brings joy and rejoicing to the heart. This highlights the dynamic nature of God's Word, suggesting that it is not a static set of principles but a vibrant and living force capable of influencing and transforming lives.

Discerning Thoughts and Intent

One of the extraordinary attributes of the Word of God is its ability to pierce into the very core of human existence. The Word can penetrate the soul and spirit, reaching the marrow, and has power to discern thoughts and intent of the heart. This profound insight into the inner workings of individuals underscores the transformative power and depth of God's Word, serving as guide for reflection and growth.

Encouragement and Assurance

Throughout the scriptures, there are statements of encouragement to remember and meditate on the words of God continually. Word of God is a source of strength, wisdom, and guidance. God assures the effectiveness of His words, emphasizing the enduring nature. Isaiah 40:8 reinforces this promise, stating that while the grass withers and the flower fades, the Word of God stands forever; a timeless and unchanging source of truth and stability.

Distinguished God's Word

In a world filled with various teachings and philosophies, the Bible warns against being swayed by cunningly devised fable words. God's words are described as pure, like a silver tried in a furnace and purified seven times.

This refinement of God's word emphasizes the unblemished and flawless nature of God's word. Discerning between genuine words of God and the deceptive words around the world is very important.

Productive God's Word

Isaiah 55:10 illustrates words of God likening to rain and snow that water the earth and bring forth growth. This statement underscores the nourishing and productive qualities of God's Word, providing sustenance for both sowing and nourishment for those who partake in it.

Authority in God's Word

Many believers have confirmed they encounter awesome power embedded in God's words. Matthew 21:21 KJV records God's words as this, "If ye have faith, and doubt not, ye shall not only do this which is done to the fig tree, but also, if ye shall say unto this mountain be thou removed, and be thou cast into the sea; it shall be done." There is authority in God's Word through Power of Faith. This statement unveils the extraordinary authority in God's words and the capability of able to move mountains and transforming circumstances.

Performance of God's Word

In the verses of Jeremiah 1:12, the Lord reveals a profound truth about God's Word. it is not merely a collection of sentiments or ideas, but a dynamic force in constant motion. The passage declares, "Then said the Lord unto me, thou hast well seen for I will hasten my word to perform it," This verse invites believers to agree and witness the active, transformative power inherent in God's promises.

Embarking on a journey into the heart of God and revelations that follows to explore significance of God's Word as an entity in perpetual motion. Beyond being a source of comfort or wisdom, it is a force actively at work, bringing changes and fulfillments in lives. In Jeremiah 1:12, "I will hasten my word to perform it." This unveils that God's Word is not a passive utterance but a dynamic, efficacious force. Unveiling God's Word as a dynamic efficacious force, not a passive utterance. God's word carries sense of urgency, purpose, and a commitment. God Almighty actively bring about the fulfillment of His promises.

Chapter 11: Dynamic Force

Mountain-Moving

Unwavering faith and Mountain-Moving Power emphasizes the authority of speaking to mountain and seeing it cast into the sea. It shows the limitless power that faith in God's word can unleash. Matthew 21:21 KJV, "Jesus answered and said unto them, Verily I say unto you, If ye have faith and doubt not, ye shall not only do this which is done to the fig tree, but also if ye shall say unto this mountain, Be thou removed, and be thou cast into the sea; it shall be done" This may be challenging, however, is possible by cultivating unwavering faith free from doubt.

Every challenge can be confronted with confidence through faith in words of God. Obstacles can be overcome, and situations can be transformed by words from the LORD. Prayer, belief, and promises of God works together. As read in Matthew 21:22 KJV which emphasizes the connection between prayer, belief, and reception. "And all things, whatsoever ye shall ask in prayer, believing, ye shall receive." Here, Jesus provides a powerful assurance that aligning prayers with unwavering belief results in the reception of all things. Matthew 21:22 reveals dynamic interplay between faith, prayer, and the fulfillment of God's promises. The verses are reminder to put faith into action.

The Word of God is of no effect if not mixed with faith underscores the necessity of faith in experiencing the full impact of God's Word. Faith transforms God's Word from passive information into dynamic, life-changing force. It is through faith believers internalize, apply, and experience the profound truths and promises in God's words.

The awesome power of God's word is not just theoretical but practical and transformative. As believers align lives with God's principles of faith, they become vessels through which God's authority are manifested and His promises are realized. In the light of Matthew 21:21-22, stand at the threshold of profound truth to the awesome power of God's words. God's word must be activated through unwavering faith and prayer. Henceforth, the verse challenges believers to live with a bold confidence in the authority bestowed in God's word knowing that through faith, mountains can be moved, and prayers can usher in the fulfillment of God's promises.

Foundational Value

This concept is rooted in scripture, particularly in Hebrews 4:2 (NIV): "For we also have had the good news proclaimed to us just as they did; but the message they heard was of no value to them, because they did not share the faith of those who obeyed. "This verse highlights that merely hearing the Word of God is not sufficient; it must be combined with faith to be effective.

Key Points of the Concept

1. Hearing vs. Believing: Hearing the Word of God alone is not enough. Belief and trust in the message are essential for it to have real impact on lives. Faith activates the power of the Word in a believer's heart.

2. **Faith as a Catalyst:** Faith acts as a catalyst that brings the promises and teachings of the Word to life. Without faith, the words remain mere text without the ability to transform or guide.

3. **Transformation Through Faith:** Faith is energizer that internalize the Word, leading to genuine spiritual transformation, moral guidance, and fulfillment of God's promises.

4. **Active Participation:** Faith represents an active response to the Word of God. It involves trust, reliance, and obedience, moving beyond passive hearing to active living.

5. **Spiritual Efficacy:** The power and efficacy of the Word are realized through faith. Faith makes the Word operational and enable it to effect changes.

6. **Promise Fulfillment:** Many of God's promises in scripture require faith for their fulfillment. Faith is the medium through which believers receive and experience God promises.

Practical Implications

1.   **Personal Application:** Believers are encouraged to not just read or hear the Word of God but to believe and apply it in their daily living. Faith turns scriptural principles into practical actions.

2.   **Trust and Confidence:** Faith builds trust and confidence in God's words and promises. Absolute trust in God's words lead to deeper more resilient living.

3.   **Growth and Maturity:** A faith-filled engagement with the Word leads to growth and maturity. It helps to navigate challenges, make ethical decisions, and grow in relationship with God.

4.   **Community and Worship:** In a community setting, shared faith in the Word of God strengthens communal bonds and fosters supportive environment for collective growth.

Illustrative Examples

1.   **Faith of Abraham:** Abraham's faith in God's promise made him the father of many nations. Despite his circumstances, his faith activated God's promise and brought it to fulfillment (Romans 4:18-21).

2.   **Healing Miracles of Jesus**: Many of Jesus' healing miracles were attributed to the faith. (Matthew 9:22, Mark 5:34). Their faith activated the healing power of Jesus' words.

Dwell Among Us

The word, "dwelt among us," Is an intentional inhabiting of the earthly realm by the Word. It means that God is not distant but intimately present and actively participating in the human experience. This dwelling among us signifies a profound closeness that defies the boundaries between God's divine presence and mortal human.

Harmonious Union

The Word of God described Jesus as the only Son of God. This glory radiates with qualities of grace and truth, emphasizing the harmonious union of divine blessings and unwavering authenticity in God's word. Believers can testify of the glory of God through His word that transcends human comprehension.

Unfailing Love and Faithfulness

God's word described God's attributes that define the very essence of God's unfailing love and faithfulness. In taking on human form, the Word exemplifies love that knows no bounds and a faithfulness that endures through all circumstances. God's word of love becomes a beacon of hope for humanity. Because God is faithful, and He is God by Himself His word must achieve the purpose He sent it forth.

The Bible, specifically from the book of Revelation chapter 14, verse 12 characterized patience and faithfulness to God's commandments as well as faith in Jesus results to actualization of God's word. It emphasizes the endurance and perseverance to realizing God's promises.

Despite trials and tribulations, God's words remain steadfast. Therefore, people need to trust God's word must surely come to pass. God's promises will surely come to pass. Those who are patient and endure are also those who faithfully follow God's words and teachings. Manifestation to God's word is not just about adhering to rules but also about having a deep and unwavering faith in Jesus and his teachings. Obedience to God's commandments or words and strong faith in Jesus Christ are very important.

Stirring the Glory

Believers are invited to behold the manifestation of God the Father and His Only Son. The scripture encourages believers to dwell and stir up their hearts with God's word and thereby encounter God's glory and transformative power in God's word.

Transformative Power

The incarnation of the Word is a testimony to the transformative power inherent in God's word. Word of God is a living reality, actively shaping the course of human history and lives. The Word made flesh becomes a catalyst for renewal, redemption, and restoration of the broken relationship between God and humanity.

Living Light

In embracing God's Word, become a call to live in the light of God reality. The transformative power of God's Word is not confined to the past but is a living force that continues to illuminate, heal, and guide those who earnestly seek to dwell in its radiance.

John 1:14 encourages believers to have deeper understanding of the transformative force embedded in God's Word. God's word is Christ, wisdom, and power of God. Jesus is made unto believers' wisdom and righteousness. Words of God carries grace, truth, and God's presence. God manifest His presence through His words. God cannot alter His words if it is sincerely embraced. Sometimes God choose to manifest His words even if not embraced.

God gives Human authority to choose to receive the word of God or not. The life-altering power of God's truth. God desire everyone to witness the glory of powerful Word of God and His transformative unfathomable power of love and faithfulness. 1 Corinthians 1:17-31 (NIV) "For Christ did not send me to baptize, but to preach the gospel, not with wisdom and eloquence, lest the cross of Christ be emptied of its power. Here, Paul is emphasizing that his main mission is to preach the gospel, not to focus on baptism or rhetoric. He wants to ensure that the power of the message of Christ's sacrifice on the cross is not overshadowed by human wisdom or eloquence.

For the message of the cross is foolishness to those who are perishing, but to us who are being saved it is the power of God. Paul explains that while some may see the message of the cross as foolishness, it represents the power of God and salvation. For it is written: "I will destroy the wisdom of the wise; the intelligence of the intelligent I will frustrate." Paul quotes from Isaiah 29:14, suggesting that human wisdom and intelligence will be confounded or made ineffective in comparison to the wisdom of God. Where is the wise person? Where is the teacher of the law? Where is the philosopher of this age? Has not God made foolish the wisdom of the world? Paul challenges the wisdom of worldly scholars, philosophers, and intellectuals, suggesting that God's wisdom surpasses human understanding.

The world, using its own wisdom, could not know God. So, God chose to save those who believe through what seems like foolishness to the world. This is the message of the cross which highlights how God's way of revealing Himself often defies human logic yet brings salvation to the world. Paul argues that despite human wisdom, people did not truly know God. It pleased God to use what may seem foolish (the preaching of the gospel) to save those who believe in Christ. Jews demand signs and Greeks look for wisdom.

Paul acknowledges the different expectations and desires of Jews and Greeks (Gentiles). Some sought miraculous signs, while others valued philosophical wisdom. Paul said, "but we preach Christ crucified: a stumbling block to Jews and foolishness to Gentiles" Despite these expectations, Paul and his companions preach Christ crucified, a message that may be offensive or foolish to some.

However, to those who are called by God, both Jews and Greeks, Christ represents both the power and wisdom of God. For the foolishness of God is wiser than human wisdom and the weakness of God is stronger than human strength. Paul emphasizes that what may seem foolish or weak from a human perspective is actually wiser and stronger than human wisdom and strength because it comes from God.

Paul said "Brothers and sisters, think of what you were when you were called. Not many of you were wise by human standards; not many were influential; not many were of noble birth." Paul reminds the Corinthians that when they were called to faith, not many of them were considered wise, influential, or noble by human standards. But God chose the foolish things of the world to shame the wise; God chose the weak things of the world to shame the strong. God deliberately chose those who were considered foolish or weak by worldly standards to shame those who thought they were wise or strong. God chose the lowly things of this world and the despised things and the things that are not to nullify the things that are.

God chose the lowly and despised things of the world, and the things that are considered nothing, to bring things that are esteemed highly by humans. so that no one may boast before him. This selection by God serves the purpose of preventing anyone from boasting before Him. It underscores that salvation and wisdom come from God not from human achievements.

It is because of him that we are in Christ Jesus who has become for us wisdom from God which is our righteousness, holiness and redemption. Paul emphasizes that it's because of God that the believers are in Christ Jesus. Christ has become for them wisdom from God, embracing righteousness, holiness, and redemption. Therefore, as it is written: "Let the one who boasts boast in the Lord. "Paul concludes by quoting from Jeremiah 9:23-24, emphasizing that if anyone boasts, they should boast in the Lord rather than in their own wisdom or accomplishments.

In this passage, Oracle of the LORD draws the contrast between wisdom of God and wisdom of the world. As Paul had emphasized that while the message of the cross may seem foolish to some, it is the power and wisdom of God surpassing human understanding and confounding worldly wisdom. This is encouragement to boast only in the Lord, no one or nothing else.

Chapter 12: Loosing Bounds

Chains of Tradition

The scripture, in Mark 7:13 caution about potential hindrance to effectiveness of God's word. "Making the word of God of none effect through your tradition, which ye have delivered: and many such like things do ye." (Mark 7:13) A caution to avoid making the word of God of no effect because of tradition. This profound statement explores the impact of traditions on the potency and accuracy of God's word. The cautionary verse serves as a timeless reminder of the vitality and accuracy of God's word if people break free from traditions that may inadvertently impede word of God impact.

Weight of Tradition

Traditions, while often rooted in cultural and religious practices can inadvertently become stumbling blocks that obstruct the pure transmission of God's word. When adherence to tradition takes precedence over a genuine understanding and application of God's word, it can dilute the transformative power of God's messages. There is a need for critical juncture where the entrenched adherence to tradition supplanted the essence of God's word. To avoid nullification or diminishing impact of God's word, though word of God is forever true. This serves as reminder that blind allegiance to customs and rituals can potentially undermine the very purpose of God's word.

Identifying Modern Traditions

In those days, it is crucial to discern which traditions may be inadvertently impeding the accurate reception and application of the word of God. This could include cultural practices, doctrinal interpretations, or rituals. Trying to indoctrinate religion practices into fundamental Christian teachings and what God says can water down the true meaning of the Word of God in some people lives.

Breaking Free from Tradition

To unleash the full power and accuracy of God's word, it is important to critically examine if a tradition is necessary and break free from traditions that hinder genuine connection with God's command. This requires a humble and open-hearted approach to the scripture, allowing it to speak directly to individuals and communities without the distortion of preconceived notions.

Embracing Living Word

God's word is dynamic and living capable of speaking directly to the hearts and minds of those who seek God's wisdom sincerely. By transcending the limitations of tradition and approaching God's word with open perspective, lead to experiencing and enjoying the transformative and liberating power inherent in the word of God.

Oracle of the LORD is a testament to the living word of God. This book encourages everyone to navigate the intricacies of faith and strive for a deeper understanding of God's word, unencumbered by rigid traditions to allow the living word of God to resonate with power and accuracy inherent in God's word.

Chapter 13: Fulfillment Despite Odds

Lessons from Sarah's Story

In the preceding paragraph, Oracle of the LORD discussed instances where it may seem that the Words of God have no effect, citing examples such as unbelief and tradition. However, it is crucial to emphasize that God's word always prevails and never fails. As illustrated in Genesis 21:1-2, where it is written, "And the Lord visited Sarah as he had said, and the Lord did unto Sarah as he had spoken. For Sarah conceived and bare Abraham a son in his old age, at the set time of which God had spoken to him."

Sarah, despite her advanced age and initial disbelief experienced the fulfillment of God's promise. This serves as a testament to the unwavering nature of God's word. It is noteworthy that God's promises often manifest even in the face of skepticism and entrenched traditions. In Sarah's case, her lack of belief did not hinder the fulfillment of God's word.

In my personal conviction, when it appears God's word has not come to pass, there might be a divine timing at play. God could be orchestrating events and awaiting the opportune moment for His promises to be realized. God's plans unfold according to His perfect timing surpassing human understanding.

Sarah's story encourages us to trust God's word, reminding us that His promises will come to pass, even when tradition or doubt may cloud our faith. We are reminded by Sarah's journey that, despite our uncertainties or delays, God's promises are unwavering and will be fulfilled in His perfect timing. The lesson from Sarah's life is to hold firm to God's word, knowing that even when circumstances seem uncertain, His promises will be realized at the appointed time.

Sarah's experience serves as a powerful reminder that God's timing is perfect. God's words and promises will be fulfilled, no matter how impossible things may seem. These versions emphasize trusting God's timing and promises, while drawing inspiration from Sarah's story.

In previous chapters, Oracle of the LORD explained in detail the following scriptures: Hebrews 4:12 "For the word of God is alive and active sharper than any double-edged sword, it penetrates even to dividing soul and spirit, joints and marrow; it judges the thoughts and attitudes of the heart."

Isaiah 55:11 "So is my word that goes out from my mouth: It will not return to me empty but will accomplish what I desire and achieve the purpose for which I sent it." This verse lays the foundation for understanding Jesus as the ultimate revelation of God. Jesus the Living Word who walked among God's people, revealing the fullness of God's character, and inviting humanity into relationship with God. The living Word of God, through Jesus Christ, the Living

Word, becomes the power of God's love and grace. Jesus restores the connection between humanity and God, offering the gift of eternal life and renewing humanity to God. Jesus embodies love, as He declares in John 14:6, "I am the way, the truth, and the life."

Law of God

The Commandments of God. In Exodus 20:1-17 "And God spoke all these words: 'I am the Lord your God" The referenced scriptures are evident that God's word surely comes into existence. This reflects the concept of God's omnipotence and that His will is instantly executed. The question of whether specific verses become true is subjective and depend on individual faith perspectives. Some scripture verses highlight different aspects of God's word, including the law, Jesus Christ, the written word, and the words proclaimed by God's prophets. God's prophecies, guidance, and commandments are timeless and applicable to all aspects of lives. While some Bible verses are understood as historical or contextual, others are considered more general and applicable to various situations throughout time.

Word Became Flesh

John 1:14 "The Word became flesh and made his dwelling among us. We have seen his glory, the glory of the one and only Son, who came from the father, full of grace and truth." In the Gospel of John, this profound statement is the essence of Jesus Christ as the embodiment of God's eternal Word taking on human form.

The Word representing the divine communication and revelation of God became a tangible reality in the person of Jesus Christ. This event is a cornerstone of Christian expressing the intimate connection between God and humans. The phrase "made his dwelling among us" is inheritance signifying that God's Word didn't merely visit or communicate from afar but chose to dwell intimately in the human existence. Jesus, as the Word incarnate, lives among people, sharing in their joys, sorrows, and challenges. The humanity of Jesus doesn't diminish his divine nature but serves as a connection between God and humanity.

The mention of "glory" signifies the divine radiance and splendor manifested in Jesus. It points to attributes of grace and truth that characterize Christ earthly ministry. The Word made flesh brought God's grace as unmerited favor and embodied the truth of God's redemptive plan for humanity. John 1:14 lays the foundation for understanding Jesus as the ultimate revelation of God, the Living Word who walked among us, revealing the fullness of God's character and invitation into relationship with God the Father, Son, and Holy Spirit. Christians believe that through Jesus Christ the Living Word, humanity can encounter the transformative power of God's love and grace.

Virtue, Faith, and Love

In a world often clouded by uncertainties, the radiant truth emanates from God's word as a guidance guiding and transforming lives through the power inherent in God's Word. 2 Peter 1:5-9 unfolds the path of Christ enrichment, revealing a sequence of virtues leading to a profound understanding of the Lord Jesus Christ.

Faith, love, and virtue are essential foundations for unlocking the hidden power in God's Word. Romans 8:4 and 10:4 are reminders of faith and trust in God's Word which are the keys to righteousness. Words of God serves as a divine guide, not only for prayer but also as a source of strength for navigating life's challenges. Let's reflect and address the misconception that God's commandments are burdensome. Romans 10:4, clarifies that Christ has already fulfilled the purpose of the law, liberating the world from impossible demands of the Law. The unattainable standards of the Law of Moses are contrasted with the accessible grace and righteousness found through faith in Christ.

Apostle Paul's teachings illuminate the centrality of love. The Law of Moses is an intricate set of commandments and regulations as described by Paul into a singular operative word called love according to Romans 13:8. This paragraph emphasizes that love fulfills the law and positions Christians on the path of righteousness. The debt of love emphasized in 1 John 4:19 is presented as the ongoing obligation that Christians carries. This is a reminder of the transformation embedded in God's Word. The absence of virtues like faith, patience, godliness, brotherly kindness, and charity can render spiritual blindness or disconnect from the purging of old sins. A life abounding in virtues becomes a fertile ground for the knowledge of the Lord Jesus Christ as is written in 2 Peter 1:8. Oracle of the LORD invites believers to explore the Word of God and embrace simplicity of faith thereby enjoying transformative power of God's love which shapes Christian landscapes.

The Power of Faith

Hebrews 4:2 in King James Version highlights fundamental truth about the effectiveness of word of God and the necessity of faith. The verse emphasizes that the Gospel was preached not only to the Hebrews but also to others. It points out a crucial distinction in the recipient of the word of God. Although the message was delivered to all, it did not yield any benefit to some because they lacked faith. This verse underscores the indispensable role of faith in receiving and benefiting from God's word. Mere exposure to the Word is insufficient. Words of God must be embraced with belief and trust. Without faith the transformative power of the Gospel remains dormant.

Faith "not being mixed with faith in them that heard it" highlights the importance of an active and receptive heart. To truly profit from the word of God, faith is utmost; not only hear it but also internalize it with unwavering faith. Faith is the catalyst that unlocks the potential of God's Word enabling it to bring about spiritual growth, transformation, and salvation.

Hebrews 4:2 serves as a reminder of the critical role faith plays in receiving the Word of God. The scripture challenges to examine one's hearts and ensure that everyone's faith is not passive but actively engaged in appropriating the truths of the Gospel into lives.

Embracing the Word with faith opens to life-changing power and experience of the fullness of God's benefits. Hebrews 4:2-3 (KJV): "For unto us was the gospel preached as well as unto them: but the word preached did not profit them not being mixed with faith in them that heard it. For we which have believed do enter into rest, as he said, As I have sworn in my wrath, if they shall enter into my rest: although the works were finished from the foundation of the world."

Now, let's analyze the passage. Verse 2: "For unto us was the gospel preached as well as unto them: but the word preached did not profit them, not being mixed with faith in them that heard it." This verse talks about the preaching of the gospel. That both the original audience and those before them had the gospel preached to them. However, it didn't benefit them because they lacked faith. The message didn't have the intended effect because they didn't believe in it.

Verse 3: "For we which have believed do enter into rest as he said. As I have sworn in my wrath, if they shall enter into my rest: although the works were finished from the foundation of the world." This emphasizes that those who believe enter a state of rest. The "rest" mentioned here refers to spiritual rest that comes with faith in God. The verse also alludes a promise of rest which is only accessible through Jesus Christ. "For he that is entered into his rest, he also hath ceased from his own works, as God did from his. Let us labor therefore to enter rest, lest any man fall after the same example of unbelief.

"For the word of God is quick, and powerful, and sharper than any two-edged sword, piercing even to the dividing asunder of soul and spirit, and of the joints and marrow, and is a discerner of the thoughts and intents of the heart." These verses highlight the importance of faith in receiving the benefits of word of God and entering Jesus paid rest provided by God. The scripture cautions against merely hearing the message without truly believing in it.

Receive Through Faith

The Power of Faith in God's words as promised in Hebrews 11:1 "Now faith is confidence in what we hope for and assurance about what we do not see." Book of Hebrews provides powerful definition of faith, emphasizing its intrinsic connection to hope and assurance. It reaffirms finding confidence in the promises in the God's word.

"Faith" goes beyond mere belief; it's described as a deep and unwavering confidence in the promises of God. It is the trust that extends beyond the tangible and the visible, reaching the unseen and the hoped-for. Faith, therefore, becomes the lens through which believers perceive and hold to assurances in God's words. Faith is never alone. The gospel of Jesus Christ means salvation by grace through faith, and faith in God always produces good works because faith is actionable. Faith is evidence of salvation and good works. This is the foundation and effect of Gospel is love. James says faith without works is dead.

Faith is motivation for generosity. The evidence of salvation produces good works. Simply believing in God doesn't lead to obedience if it doesn't lead to love and transformation. "Oracle of the LORD" is birthed by faith through love of God.

The concept of hope is vital in receiving the fullness of God's promises. Faith is not blind; rather it is confident expectation in the fulfillment of God's promises. The words of God encompass various scriptures and divine revelations and serves as the foundation for hope. Believers find assurance in the words of God trusting that what has been promised will come to pass even if it is not immediately visible. This is significant in highlighting the dynamic power of faith. It involves an active and enduring trust in God's promises, regardless of present circumstances or visible evidence. It is through such faith that believers claim word of God, finding strength, comfort, and direction during life's challenges.

The "power" of faith lies in its transformative impact on the lives and finding sources of resilience, peace, and guidance. Power of faith is derived from profound trust in the reliability and faithfulness of God as revealed in the God's word. Acts 19:20, says, "So mightily grew the word of God and prevailed," This verse reflects the unstoppable and transformative power in God's word as it spread throughout Ephesus and beyond during the early days of Christianity. This verse emphasizes several key aspects of the power of God's word.

1. **Unstoppable Growth:**

    The phrase "mightily grew" indicates that the word of God was spreading rapidly and with great strength. Despite any opposition or challenges, the message of the gospel continued to reach more and more people. This growth wasn't just in numbers, but in the depth of understanding and the transformative effect it had on individuals and communities.

2. **Prevailing Power:**

    The word "prevailed" means that God's word overcame obstacles and triumphed over all resistances. In Ephesus, this included overcoming the influence of idolatry, magic, and other spiritual and cultural forces that were prevalent in the city. The gospel's power was greater than any other belief or practice leading to significant cultural and spiritual shift.

3. **Transformative Impact:**

    The verse also points to the transformative nature of God's word. As it spread, it changed lives, leading people to abandon old ways and embrace new life in Christ. The power of God's word was not just theoretical but had a real, tangible impact on the lives of those who heard and accepted it.

5. **Endurance and Resilience:**

>This verse highlights the enduring God's word. No matter the challenges or opposition, the word of God cannot be extinguished. It continues to grow and prevail shaping history and individual lives alike.

6. **Divine Authority:**

>This underscores that the power of God's word is rooted in divine authority. It is not merely human wisdom or persuasion that caused it to grow and prevail, but the very power of God working through it. This divine backing ensures that God's word will accomplish what it sets out to do.

Acts 19:20 speaks to the unwavering, powerful, and prevailing God's word. It is a reminder that God's truth once proclaimed cannot be stopped or silenced and it will continue to grow, transform, and overcome all opposition.

Chapter 14: Heavens Came to Existence

God's Breath.

Breath of God adds layers of depth to the creative power of God. The breath of God's mouth confirms effortless and awe-inspiring creation. The stars were brought into existence with a single breath of God. Breath of God is as powerful as God's words. The ultimate words of God the Creator whose word has the power to bring to existence and shape the wonders of Heaven and Earth. God's word manifests majesty, authority, and transcendence above all names. God's powerful words continue bringing to remembrance the origin and sustainability power of God.

Isaiah 55:11 "So is my word that goes out from my mouth: It will not return to me empty but will accomplish what I desire and achieve the purpose for which I sent it." This verse was quoted in earlier pages of this book as reference to where God's invitation to seek Him and His ways is extended to all people. Isaiah 55 emphasizes the power and reliability of God's word, comparing it to the efficacy of rain and snow in causing growth on the earth. This verse highlights the effectiveness of God's word. In the same way rain and snow accomplish the purpose of nourishing the earth. God's word is actively going forth from His mouth to bring about intended results.

Meaningful Returns

Meaningful returns affirm the certainty and completeness of God's word. Unlike human words that may fall short or fail to achieve their intended purpose. God's word never returns without accomplishing its purpose. Every word of God is full of meaning and efficacy. Isaiah 55 concludes with powerful affirmation of the divine intentionality behind every God's word. God's word is not arbitrary; it is purposeful and effective. Whatever God desires and intends to achieve through His word will come to fruition.

Purposeful and effective

There is authority and reliability of God's word. God's word is not empty or void of meaning. God's word carries inherent power to bring about the intended outcome. The scripture encourages believers to trust in the potency of God's word, recognizing it as a force that accomplishes His divine purposes on Earth. Isaiah 55:11 serves as a source of comfort and assurance affirms the trustworthiness of God's promises and the effectiveness of God's word.

Affirmed God's Word

The transformative God's Word is beyond human understanding. God's word can restore, renew, redeem, and make all things new again. Many believers trust the profound capabilities of Word of God and believe the ability to restore, renew, redeem, and make all things new. God's words are not mere promises but transformative reality that affirmed through the scriptures and resonates in earth.

The process of restoration begins with the Word of God acting as a healing balm for the wounded soul. It is a force that can mend the brokenness within, bringing comfort to the afflicted and solace to the distressed. The promises embedded in the scriptures serve as beacons of hope, assuring that through faith and connection to the Word, one's sense of purpose and well-being can be restored.

God's Word Revitalizes

Mind renewal is another facet of the Words of God. God's words carry effective influence in believer's mind. God's word can revitalize mind, spirit, and perspective. By immersing oneself in the Word, a transformative renewal occurs as shedding of old ways, attitudes, and perspectives. The Word has the power to rejuvenate the weary, offering fresh outlook on life and renewed sense of purpose. Words of God is the truth.

The scripture says, "you will know the truth, the truth will set you free" This is what the Oracle of God represents. He that dwelleth in the secret of the Most High shall abide under the shadow of the Almighty God. Redemption is a central theme in Christianity which finds its roots in the redemptive power of God's Word.

The scriptures reveal the grace and forgiveness, showcasing how the Word can redeem even the most broken and lost aspects of human existence. Through faith in the Word, individuals can experience a profound sense of redemption, liberation from guilt, and renewed opportunity for life of righteousness.

The culmination transformative process is the ability of the Word to make all things new. This is not a mere symbolic gesture but a promise of salvation and regeneration. The Word of God, as a creative force, has the capacity to transform lives, circumstances, and perspectives, ushering in new chapter of hope, purpose, and divine alignment. In essence, the Word of God stands as a dynamic force, actively working to restore what is broken, renew what is weary, redeem what is lost, and make all things new. Embracing this truth invites believers into a continual journey of transformation, guided by the timeless and transcendent power of God's Word.

Transcendent God's Word

The transcendent power of God's word is an awe-inspiring force, capable of restoring the soul instantly. Psalm 23:3 beautifully captures this essence, declaring, "He restores my soul; He leads me in the paths of righteousness for His name's sake." This verse stands as a testament to the profound impact Word of God have on humanity, bringing renewal that surpasses human understanding. The scriptures are referred to as living Word of God which possesses unparalleled ability to transform and restore lives.

Hebrews 4:12 provides insights into the depth of transformative power in God's word; stating, "For the Word of God is living and powerful, and sharper than any two-edged sword, piercing even to the dividing asunder of soul and spirit, and of the joints and marrow and is a discerner of thoughts and intents of hearts "Faith, love, and virtue are essential foundations for unlocking the hidden power in God's Word. Romans 8:4 and 10:4 is a reminder that simple faith and trust in God's Word are the keys to righteousness. The scripture serves as divine guide, not only for prayer but also as a source of strength to navigate life's challenges." This verse illustrates the Word's precision in address intricate layers of humanity, a discerning force that cuts through the barriers of despair and darkness.

Oracle of the LORD have witnessed the profound impact of God's word in some circumstances. The Word of God serves as an effective weapon against despair, offering not just solace but genuine restoration. It has the ability to renew minds, redeem souls, and make all things new. The transformative journey is not just a one-time event but a continual process, where the Word of God works, shaping thoughts, intentions, and ultimately guiding the path of righteousness.

The Word of God stands as a beacon of hope, a source of transformation, and a medium for soul restoration. Embracing the scriptures with an open heart and seeking the inerrant words of God leads to experiencing a profound and enduring power that can make lasting impacts on lives.

Timeless Wisdom

Proverbs 3:5-6 offers a profound and timeless directive that transcends the limitations of human

understanding, urging believers to place unwavering trust in the LORD. The verses read: "Trust in the Lord with all your heart and lean not on your own understanding; in all your ways submit to God and he will make your paths straight."
In a world often marked by uncertainty and complexities, these verses serve as a beacon of guidance, a call to surrender anxieties and uncertainties to God Almighty. The command to trust in the LORD with all your heart affirmed deep faith that extends beyond mere acknowledgment. It is a call to wholeheartedly rely on the divine wisdom and sovereignty of God.

The caution against leaning on one's own understanding confirms the limited perspective of human wisdom compared to the omniscient knowledge of the Creator. Human understanding, though valuable is finite and subject to the constraints of time and circumstance. By contrast, trusting in the LORD's word is an invitation to tap into the boundless wisdom of a transcendent God whose understanding surpasses all comprehension.

The promise embedded in Proverbs 3:5-6 verses are powerful and reassuring. "He will make your paths straight." This is divine guidance and alignment to God's word when one submits to God in all aspects of life. The Word of God, as mentioned in Proverbs 3:5-6, is a timeless source of wisdom that remains relevant in every era, offering a blueprint for navigating life's journey with confidence and purpose.

Embracing the message of proverbs 3:5-6 involves a continual surrender of one's will to God Almighty, acknowledging the limitations of human understanding and trusting in the overarching plan and purpose of a transcendent God. There is solace, direction, and sense of purpose in navigating the intricacies of life guided by the powerful, timeless, and transcendent Word of God.

Creative God's Word

The Word of God stands as the masterful peace bringing forth creation to reality. This resonates in the scriptures, where Luke 1:37 declares, "For with God nothing shall be impossible." This further affirmed in Hebrews 11:3, stating, "By faith, we understand that the world was created by the word of God." This profound truth confirms the transformative power inherent in God's word, which not only shapes the world but also elicits obedience to God's command.

The Bible consistently emphasizes the potency of God's word as a force that brings things into existence. The very act of creation, as described in Genesis refers to God command, "Let there be," illustrating the foundational principle that God's word has creative authority. The Bible consistently emphasizes the potency of God's word as a force that brings things into existence. The very act of creation as described in Genesis refers to God's command, "Let there be," illustrating the foundational principle that God's word has creative authority. Hebrews 11:3 serves as reinforcements of creation affirming that the world was formed by the word of God drawing attention to the invisible world behind the visible. This insight challenges believers to perceive the world through the lens of faith recognizing the unseen hand that shapes the world reality

Chapter 15: God's Principles

Actionable Faith

Sara's story, as recounted in Hebrews 11:11, exemplifies the synergy between faith and the creative power of God's word. Despite being past the age of childbearing, Sara received strength through faith and bore a child. This illustrates the transformative influence of trusting in the faithfulness of God's promises. Embracing the transformative power of God's word and aligning with God's words open doors to miraculous possibilities. With God nothing is impossible. God makes invisible becomes visible, and the impossible becomes attainable in the atmosphere of faith.

Scripture specifically confirmed the God's word and his relationship with humanity in 2 Peter 3:9, "The Lord is not slack concerning his promise" refers to the fact that God is not slow or negligent in fulfilling the promises he has made to humanity. It's reassurance that God's promises will come to pass, even if it may seem delayed from a human perspective. "As some men count slackness" implies that some people might interpret God's apparent delay in fulfilling his promises as indifference or negligence on his part. However, the verse continues to explain that this is not the case.

"But is longsuffering to us-ward" that instead of being slow or indifferent, God is patient endures with humanity. God apparent delays is not a sign of neglect, but rather a display of his patience and mercy towards humanity. The verse concludes with the reason behind this patience: "not willing that any should perish, but that all should come to repentance." This means that God's delay is not because he wants anyone to be lost or to suffer, but because he desires that all people have the opportunity to turn away from their wrongdoing (repent) and find salvation. God makes invisible becomes visible, and the impossible becomes attainable in atmosphere of faith. The transformative power of God's word and alignment with God's commands opens doors to miraculous possibilities. In essence, this verse emphasizes God's faithfulness to his promises, his patience with humanity, and his desire for everyone to have the opportunity to repent and be saved.

Mercy Pathway

Understanding the divine path as an avenue of mercy according to the psalmists: "All the paths of the LORD are mercy unto those who keep His commandments." This acknowledgment of God's commands as the source of creation emphasizes a harmonious relationship between obedience and the unfolding of divine mercy. The interplay between God's word, faith, and obedience unveils the powerful words of God Almighty. Understanding God's divine path as an avenue of mercy as declared by the psalmists "All the paths of the LORD are mercy unto those who keep His commandments." This acknowledgment of God's word emphasizes a harmonious relationship between

God and humanities for the sake of God unfolding divine mercy.

God's Principles

The scriptures encourage believers to align their action with God's principle in journey of transformation harmonizes effectiveness with profound principles laid out by the scripture. Going deeper into the words of God can sometimes bring challenges and triumphs. God is a righteous God and expect His children to live righteously for deeper connection with God. Word of God is a guiding principle for Christian journey, providing a roadmap for understanding and pursuing God's righteousness. Holy Spirit is the enablement because of human weakness. Humans make strong and righteous through the power of the Holy Spirit.

Obedience and Righteousness

Living in accordance with God's principles involves embracing obedience. Through obedience, believers walk in the path of righteousness. The challenges and triumphs encountered on this journey contribute to the refinement of character, fostering profound connection with God's divine plan. This passage serves as encouragement and guidance, illuminating the path towards a deeper connection with God and the pursuit of His righteousness. Applying God's Principle daily enable believers to connect to God.

The challenges, triumphs, and timeless wisdom found in the scriptures serves as vivid picture of transformative power of obedience and righteousness.

Devine Wisdom

Earthly wisdom is deferent from the omnipotent wisdom of God. John 5:5 affirmed God's power exceeds earthly wisdom. "Who is he that overcomes the world, he that believes that Jesus is the Son of God." The starting journey to Divine wisdom is to believe firstly that Jesus is the Son of God. Matthew 4:4: "Jesus answered, 'It is written: 'Man shall not live on bread alone, but on every word that comes from the mouth of God. There are numerous verses in the Bible that emphasize the importance of trusting in God's wisdom. Not relying on mere words of human for guidance and wisdom. Wisdom of God is profitable. This sets the stage for exploring the supernatural possibility through God's transformative word.

Job's life becomes a compelling illustration of the transformative power of God's word. Though regarded as forsaken by human standards, God's word declared otherwise. Despite immense loss, God's faithfulness led to supernatural deliverance and complete restoration for Job. This is a testament to God's ability to turn adversity into abundance.

Drawing from Job's story, the narrative emphasizes that God's word holds the power to deliver and restore. The assurance that God can turn situations around is a key takeaway in Oracle of the LORD. By aligning with God's principles, believers find hope and refuge in the transformative power of God's word. The Word of God stands as the masterful peace bringing forth creation to reality. This resonates in Luke 1:37, "For with God nothing shall be impossible." Also, in Hebrews 11:3, stating, "By faith, we understand that the world was created by the word of God." This profound truth confirms the transformation inherent in God's word which shapes the world.

Chapter 16: Revealing Power

Hidden Mystery

Apostle Paul emphasizes the transformative God's word as revelation in Colossians 1:25-27. As a minister entrusted with the dispensation of God's message, Paul highlights the unveiling of mystery that was previously concealed but is now made manifest to the world. This revelation brings forth profound implications, particularly in understanding the essence of Christ as offers of hope for humanity.

Paul begins by acknowledging his role as a minister chosen by God to fulfill His word. The dispensation of God's message is not merely a duty, but a divine commission entrusted to Paul for the benefit of many. This divine dispensation illustrates the significance of God's word as a vehicle for revelation. Word of God carries the power to illuminate humans' hearts and minds.

Paul goes on to describe the mystery that was concealed for ages and generations but is now unveiled to believers. This is the revelation of Christ among the Gentiles. The unveiling of this mystery represents a pivotal moment in God's plan of salvation, extending His grace and redemption beyond the confines of a particular ethnicity or culture, but the whole world.

The Riches of Glory

Central to the revelation of this mystery is the profound truth that Christ resides within believers, serving as the source of hope and glory. This indwelling presence of Christ transcends human comprehension, offering a glimpse into the richness of God's glory manifesting among His people. It is through this revelation that believers are invited to deeper communion with God through God's word thereby experiencing His transformative power.

The revelation of "Christ within us" carries significant implications for Christian journey. It instills a sense of hope amidst life's challenges, as written in the scripture God's presence through Christ dwelling within God's people. Evidence of transformative power of God manifests when lives are align with God's word in thoughts, words, and deeds.

The passage from Colossians underscores the profound significance of God's word as revelation. It reveals the mystery of Christ dwelling within, offering hope and glory amidst life's uncertainties. As recipients of this revelation and grace through Jesus Christ are called to embrace the transformative power of God's word to illuminate their hearts, minds, and manifest His glory.

Valley of Dry Bones.

Ezekiel 37:1-13 (NIV) says, "The hand of the Lord was on me, and he brought me out by the Spirit of the Lord and set me in the middle of a valley; it was full of bones. He led me back and forth among them, and I saw great many bones on the floor of the valley, bones that were very dry. He asked me, "Son of man, can these bones live?" I said, "Sovereign Lord, you alone know. "Then he said to me, "Prophesy to these bones and say to them, 'Dry bones, hear the word of the Lord! This is what the Sovereign Lord says to these bones: I will make breath enter you, and you will come to life. I will attach tendons to you and make flesh come upon you and cover you with skin; I will put breath in you, and you will come to life. Then you will know that I am the Lord."

So, I prophesied as I was commanded. And as I was prophesying, there was a noise, a rattling sound, and the bones came together, bone to bone. I looked, and tendons and flesh appeared on them, and skin covered them, but there was no breath in them.

Then he said to me, "Prophesy to the breath; prophesy, son of man, and say to it, 'This is what the Sovereign Lord says: Come, breath, from the four winds and breathe into these slain, that they may live." So, I prophesied as he commanded me, and breath entered them; they came to life and stood up on their feet a vast army. Then he said to me: "Son of man, these bones are the people of Israel. They say, 'Our bones are dried up and our hope is gone; we are cut off.' Therefore, prophesy and say to them: 'This is what the Sovereign Lord says: My people, I am going to open your graves and bring you up from them; I will bring you back to the land of Israel. Then you, my people, will know that I am the Lord, when I open your graves and bring you up from them.

Ezekiel's vision of the valley of dry bones is a powerful testament to the restoration and resurrection power of God. In this passage, Ezekiel finds himself in the midst of a valley filled with bones that are not just dead, but very dry signifying a state of complete hopelessness and desolation.

God prompts Ezekiel to prophesy to these bones, to speak life into them. Despite the apparent impossibility of the situation, Ezekiel obeys, demonstrating his faith in God's ability to bring life out of death. As Ezekiel prophesies, there were miraculous responses from the bones as they begin to rattle and come together, forming skeletons, then tendons, flesh, and skin. However, they remain lifeless until the breath of God is invoked upon them.

This passage symbolizes the restoration of God's people. The bones represent the people in a state of spiritual and national death, scattered and hopeless. But through Ezekiel's prophecy, God promises to breathe new life into them, to restore them as God's people, nation, and to bring them back to their land. It's a promise of resurrection from the depths of despair, a declaration that even when all seems lost, God's power to restore and revive is limitless.

The message extends beyond the ancient Israelites to all who feel spiritually dead or hopeless. It's a reminder that God can breathe life into the driest of bones, that His power to restore and renew knows no bounds. No matter how desolates the circumstances may seem, God's promise of restoration stands firm, offering hope and new life to all who trust in Him.

Chapter 17: Embracing His Power

Assurance Transcend Boundaries

God establishes His Words. Words of God are timeless assurance that transcends the boundaries of time and circumstance. God delights on unwavering nature of His's promises. Every word from the LORD is destined to come to fruition. If in fact, it is a word from Almighty God. God's word is trustworthy and reliable. There is a song that says, "I take Him at His word, I believe it and so is" There are trustworthiness and reliability inherent in the word of God. God establishes His Word and commits to bring it to pass. There is covenantal bond between the Creator and creation. Word of God become unshakable foundation upon which the course of events unfolds in humanity.

The certainty of God's Word instills a profound sense of confidence among those believe in God's word. This testifies the consistency of God's word, highlighting the faithfulness with which He honors His promises. The divine commitment for God to fulfill His Word becomes a source of hope for fostering deeper trust in the reliability of God's word.

In the midst of life's uncertainties, understanding God's Word will undoubtedly come to pass serves as an anchor for faithfulness to His word. This assurance enables those who believe in God's word to trust on promises of God, even when circumstances seem otherwise. This is a call for unwavering trust in God's word knowing that God will surely deliver as promised.

In practical terms, embracing the assurance that God establishes His Word encourages believers to align their lives with God's word. This shows God reliability to God's unwavering promises. This steadfast trust in God's word fosters a sense of assurance that God's Word is a firm foundation upon which to build life confidently.

Inherent in Words

God's Words are accurate, truthful, and unwavering commitment to fulfillment. The power inherent in words cannot return void but must accomplish the purpose for which it sent. Oracle of the LORD reveals the significance of God's words and the transformative impact on the lives of those who believe. The words of God are true and certain.

Psalm 33 is a song of praise that acknowledges God's sovereignty, faithfulness, and the reliability of His word. The verse in its entirety is often rendered as: "For the word of the Lord is right and true; he is faithful in all he does." (Psalm 33:4, NIV)

"Is right": "right" means morally correct, just, and true. It emphasizes the reliability, trustworthiness, and ethical God's word. God's word leads to righteousness and aligns with what is just and good.

Moral Guidance: It implies that God's word provides a solid foundation for moral decisions and behavior.

Reliability: It is assurance to trust God's promises and instructions. God's words are always correct and beneficial.

Divine Wisdom: It highlights that God's wisdom and knowledge are perfect and surpass human understanding Psalm 33:4, serves as an encouragement to trust on God's words. It reassures that following God's word will lead to inherently good and just. "For the word of God is right" conveys that God's word is a reliable, ethical, and trustworthy source of guidance. It reflects the belief that living according to God's word aligns to just and true.

Cannot Return Void

Word of God must accomplish what is sent for. This statement aligns with God's power and effectiveness. Isaiah 55:11 has been referenced multiple times in this book as one of the powerful verses regarding God's word "so is my word that goes out from my mouth will not return to me empty but will accomplish what I desire and achieve the purpose for which I sent it." The bible described Words of God like rain falling on the ground and cannot return empty. God's words do not return in vain but bring changes and growths.

God the Scriptwriter

God knows the beginning of the stories and how the stories will end. This confirmed God's plan and sovereignty as the scriptwriter of existence.

God's word aligns with predestination and God's omniscience, knowing the beginning from the end. This is why words of God are always correct at all seasons. The scripture calls it "sincere milk" This emphasizes the timeless and unchanging nature of God's words. The reference to "sincere milk" comes from 1 Peter 2:2. "crave pure spiritual milk", so that people will grow up in salvation. 1 Peter 2:2 (NIV): "Like newborn babies, crave pure spiritual milk so that by it you may grow up in your salvation."

Energy through Revelation

Ezekiel 2:2, depicts a profound moment where the spirit entered Ezekiel upon hearing the word of God, empowering him and enabling him to receive divine revelation. This passage illuminates the inherent energy and power contained within God's word, which transcends mere language and conveys transformative force. Indeed, "God's word carries a high level of energy".

The energy inherent in God's word is not merely metaphorical; it operates on a cosmic level, affecting both the spiritual and physical realms. Energy in God's word is dynamic and potent and capable of producing tangible effects in the lives of believers and the world at large. Just as electricity slings through wires, God's word surges with divine power sparking awakening, healing, and revelation.

Moreover, the verse affirmed that God's word possesses the capacity to unveil truths that resonate deeply within the hearts. It penetrates the soul, stirring emotions, illuminating the mind, and inspiring action.

Energy in word of God manifests through the heart of receivers, emphasizes the intimate and powerful God's word.

Ezekiel's experience of being set upon his feet means the transformative impact of encountering God's word. It signifies empowerment, strength, and a sense of purpose bestowed upon receivers through the indwelling of the Holy Spirit. Just as Ezekiel was enabled to stand firm and attentive before the LORD, so too power in God's words empowered people to heed the voice of God and carry out His will.

Ezekiel 2:2 serves as expressive reminder of the extraordinary power contained within God's word. It's an invitation to approach scripture with reverence and expectation, recognizing its potential to energize, transform, and illuminate. Those who have been impacted by the Word of God recognizes the transformative power of God's words.

Lessons from the Blind Beggar

Luke 18:35-39, talks about the story of a blind beggar who despite societal rebuke and hindrances, persists in his faith and earnestly cries out to Jesus for mercy. The story serves as a profound testament to the transformative power of unwavering belief and relentless perseverance in the face of adversity. The blind beggar, positioned at the roadside, hears the commotion of a passing multitude and learns of Jesus' presence. Though he cannot see Jesus with his physical eyes, he possesses an unwavering conviction in the healing power of the Son of David. His faith transcends physical sight and ignites a fervent plea for mercy.

Remarkably, when confronted with discouragement and rebuke from those around him, the blind beggar does not waver. Instead, he amplifies his cry for help, undeterred by the opinions of others. His persistence serves as a powerful example of resolute faith in action. Upon encountering Jesus, the blind beggar's faith was richly rewarded. He received the miraculous gift of sight in an instant and his life was forever changed. Notably, his response to those who question the source of his healing is marked by simplicity and conviction. He declares, "All I know is that I was blind, but now I see. Jesus, the Son of David, healed me."

This story holds profound relevance for journey to salvation. Like the blind beggar, anyone may encounter obstacles and doubts along the path of faith. Yet, Oracle of the LORD, calls for persistency in belief, trusting in the power and mercy of God. It is a reminder that true faith is not swayed by external circumstances or the opinions of others but remains steadfast in its pursuit of divine intervention.

Furthermore, the blind beggar's unwavering testimony underscores the transformative nature of encountering Jesus. His healing serves as a tangible manifestation of God's grace and mercy. Is an inspiration to people to embrace the transformative power of Christ.

Ultimately, the story of the blind beggar serves as a challenge to believers inspiring them to cultivate faith that perseveres in the face of adversity and to trusts in unwaveringly God's promises. God ensures His goodness and mercy to the world. Like the blind beggar, people will be blessed if persistently cry out to Jesus for mercy, knowing that He is faithful to answer and transform lives according to His will.

Chapter 18: Unlocking Wisdom of God

Power, Grace, and Glory

In Matthew 13:9-13, Jesus speaks in parables, revealing profound truths about the kingdom of heaven to the hearer. This passage serves as a powerful illustration of the manner in which God imparts His wisdom to humanity. There is manifestation of God's power, grace, and glory in His word. The way words of God manifest transcends human comprehension. Just as Jesus spoke in parables to convey Devine truths, God communicates His wisdom through various means. Discerning words of God require a receptive heart and a willingness to seek Him diligently.

God's people are endowed with the privilege of accessing the wisdom of God as outlined in 1 Corinthians 2:9, which declares that "these things are freely given unto us." However, the realization of this wisdom necessitates a proactive pursuit. That is why the scripture inspires readers to diligently seeking divine revelation. James 1:21-22 KJV "Wherefore lay apart all filthiness and superfluity of naughtiness, and receive with meekness the engrafted word, which is able to save your souls. But be ye doers of the word, and not hearers only, deceiving your own selves"

Ultimately, unlocking the wisdom of God is a journey of intimacy with the Creator. It is a process of continual seeking, praying, and surrendering to pursue a deeper understanding of God's ways. God's guidance permeate position people to experience fullness of God's power, grace, and glory.

Illuminate Hearts and Mind

It is important to humbly acknowledge the finite depth of God's word. The scripture encourages people to fervently pray for the Spirit of wisdom, revelation, and understanding to illuminate their hearts and minds. Through God's gracious intervention, believers can grasp the profound mysteries of God's divine plan and purpose. Tapping into the wisdom of God involves faith and prioritization.

It requires shifting from relying solely on human intellect, strength, and reasoning to embrace faith and fully reliance on God's guidance. This requires surrendering preconceived notions and opening hearts to the leading of the Holy Spirit to perceive the hidden truths embedded within God's word and discern His voice amidst the clamor of the world.

Understanding God's Timing

There are times God's timing appears mysterious. At times some prayers may seem unanswered and promises unfulfilled. Yet, amidst the waiting, there lies deeper truth. God's delay does not equate to denial. Instead, it serves a purpose, often leading to greater good and fulfillment of His divine plan.

Zechariah 1:6 offers insight into this divine timing, that God is faithful to His Word and His unwavering commitment to fulfill His decrees. Despite the apparent delay to answer prayers, His promises remain steadfast, overtaking the course of history and prevailing over generations.

At times, God delays His answer to prayers or the fulfillment of His Word for reasons beyond understanding. These delays may serve to refine faith, strengthen character, or align circumstances according to His perfect will. Like a master craftsman intricately weaving threads of purpose, God orchestrates events in His time for the ultimate display of His glory.

Consider the story of Joseph in the Old Testament. Despite enduring years of hardship and seemingly unanswered prayers, God's timing was perfect. Through Joseph's journey from the pit to the pinnacle of power, God's divine plan unfolded saving him from famine to fulfilling God promises.

Similarly, God's delays are not arbitrary but purposeful. Delay is not denial, it may lead to trust in God sovereignty, even when the path ahead seems uncertain. Oracle of the LORD inspires readers to wait upon the Lord and remain steadfast in faith, knowing that God's timing is impeccable and His plans are for good not for harm. Jeremiah 29:11 KJV "For I know the thoughts that I think toward you, saith the Lord, thoughts of peace, and not of evil, to give you an expected end."

In the waiting, there is comfort in the words of Isaiah 40:31, "But they who wait for the Lord shall renew their strength, they shall mount up with wings like eagles, they shall run and not be weary; they shall walk and not faint." There is solace in God's perfect timing knowing that His delays are not denial but rather testament to His unfailing love and wisdom.

Incontestable Authority

In a world filled with opinions and suggestions, there exists God's unwavering authority. The Word of God is steadfast. Unlike human thoughts or opinions, God's Word stands as the ultimate representation of God's authority. It is not subject to debate or interpretation but serves as the very expression of God's mind. Hebrews 12:2 is a reminder to fix eyes on the author and finisher of faith, none other than Jesus Christ Himself. In Him and through His Word is strength in time of needs. Just as a skilled author crafts a story from the depths of imagination, so too does God use His Word to script things into existence.

Psalm 62:11 declares, the unmatched power inherent in God's Word. It is not merely a collection of letters or phrases but manifestation of God's power, authority and sovereignty. "God has spoken once, twice have I heard this: that power belongs unto God." These words resonate with a resounding truth and emphasizes the supremacy of God's Word above all.

John 15:7, further illuminates the transformative power of dwelling in God's Word. Jesus Himself assures the reason to abide in Him and allow His Word to dwell richly in us. When we abide solemn in Christ and align our desires with His will, there will be fulfillment. This statement affirms the intimate connection between abiding in Christ and experiencing the fulfillment of His power as a testament to the authority and efficacy of God's Word.

In a world where uncertainty abounds and opinions clashes sometimes, anchor firmly in the unshakable truth of God's Word. It may not always conform to human understanding, but its life-giving power that transcends comprehension. With Jesus as the author and His Word as the guiding light, anyone can confidently navigate life's uncertainties, knowing that God's Word is not merely a suggestion but the very essence of divine authority and guidance.

Unwavering Promise and Sovereignty

God's sovereignty is an eternal truth that reveal throughout the scriptures and through the ages. In Isaiah 14:24, the prophet Isaiah summarizes the essence of the assurance of God's word "The LORD of hosts hath sworn, saying, surely as I have thought, so shall it come to pass; and as I have purposed, so shall it stand." (Isaiah 14:24)

This verse unveils the majestic authority of God, the Creator of the whole Worls, whose thoughts transcend time and space, whose purposes endure through eternity. This verse confirms the unshakeable foundation of God's promises. God's promises are grounded not in fleeting human intentions but in the immutable will of the Almighty.

"The LORD of hosts hath sworn", this statement resonates with the weight of certainty. God's word reflect a covenantal commitment, a solemn oath that emanates from the very essence of God's character. When the LORD affirms it, is as good as done, for His word is the pinnacle of truth, unblemished by the frailties of mortal existence.

"Surely as I have thought, so shall it come to pass," here lies the assurance of fulfillment. Every God's word, every scripture, and revelation is directed to the well-being of humanity. God's thoughts are not bound by the constraints of uncertainty. Words of God are the blueprint of providence, guiding the course of events with unfailing precision.

"And as I have purposed, so shall it stand" embodies the unwavering resolve of the Almighty. His purposes are not subject to the whims of circumstance, or the caprice of mortal will. They stand as unassailable monuments of divine determination and immovable in the face of adversity.

Many have testified to the redemptive power of God's word and have witnessed the fulfillment of His promises and salvation. God's word remains steadfast, a beacon of hope in times of uncertainty. Countless people continue to find solace in the unchanging sovereignty of God. The oracle of the Lord encourages us, in the midst of life's storms, to anchor our faith in the bedrock of God's promises, trusting that He who has promised is faithful to fulfill every word."

Oracle of the LORD stand firm in the assurance of God's unfailing love, trusting in the LORD of hosts whose word endures forever. The following chapters that follow explore some practical instance of passions, values, and purpose that define Godly characters.

Chapter 19: Practical Christian Living

Manifestations of God's Word

God's Word in Exodus 23:22, promises protection, guidance, and blessings to humanity. This verse underscores the profound impact of obedience to God's word as a transformative force that entreats intervention. Luke 5:5 KJV, "And Simon answering said unto him, Master, we have toiled all the night, and have taken nothing: nevertheless, at thy word I will let down the net" This verse occurs in the Gospel of Luke, in the New Testament. The scene takes place by the Lake of Gennesaret (also known as the Sea of Galilee). Jesus was teaching a crowd, and Simon Peter (referred to as Simon here) has been fishing all night without success.

"And Simon answering said unto him" Simon Peter responded to Jesus. Jesus has given a command or made a request to which Simon replied. "Master" Simon addresses Jesus with respect, recognizing Him as a teacher or someone with authority. "We have toiled all the night and have taken nothing" Simon explains their situation. He and the other fishermen have worked hard all night but have caught no fish. This highlights their exhaustion and the futility of their efforts. "Nevertheless, at thy word I will let down the net" Despite their lack of success and probable skepticism, Simon decides to obey Jesus' instruction. The phrase "at thy word" shows Simon's faith and willingness to trust Jesus' word surpasses his own experience. This verse shows powerful moment of faith and obedience. Simon Peter, an experienced fisherman, knows that fishing during the day (especially after a fruitless night) is typically not productive. Yet, he chooses to act on Jesus' command. This highlights the enduring relevance and potency of God's Word in shaping lives and outcomes.

Lessons and Reflections

This the power of faith and trust in Jesus. Simon's decision to follow Jesus' instruction, despite his own doubts and professional knowledge, demonstrates deep trust. This serves as encouragement to rely on Jesus' guidance, even when it contradicts own understanding. Simon's response shows the importance of obedience to God's word. The willingness to act on Jesus' instruction without questioning it reflects a profound faith.

Persistence and Effort.

The verse also subtly highlights the virtues of perseverance and hard work. Despite having worked all night without results, Simon is willing to try again at Jesus' command. Such moment sets the stage for the miraculous catch of fish that follows, illustrating that success and provision come from God. Human effort alone is not always sufficient and God's intervention is crucial. The message from this verse is inspiring. It teaches the value of trusting in God's word and timing, persisting in efforts even when results are not immediately visible. The is the readiness to obey divine instructions over personal expertise or logic.

Luke 5:5 "And Simon answering said unto him, Master, we have toiled all the night, and have taken nothing: nevertheless at thy word I will let down the net" is a testament to the power of faith and obedience.

Prophetic Fulfillment

Exodus emphasizes the certainty of God's promises. God's Word is inherently powerful and efficacious. Here is another verse that confirms authority in God's word "Surely as I have thought, so shall it come to pass" emphasizes the divine authority behind every word of God. This assurance extends beyond mere words and encompass the fulfillment of prophetic declarations, illustrating the efficacy of God's Word in shaping events and circumstances according to God's will.

In Acts 24:14-16, the apostle Paul defended himself before Felix, the Governor of Judea, against accusations brought by Jewish leaders. Paul begins by acknowledging that he follows the teachings of Jesus Christ, which some people may view as heresy. Despite this label, Paul declares his unwavering devotion to God, affirming his belief in everything written in the Law and the Prophets according to the scriptures.

Paul's faith is grounded in the divine authority in God's word, as revealed through the Scriptures and the Prophets. Paul emphasizes his hope in God 's word. The resurrection Paul explanation is not limited to the righteousness alone but extends to both the just and the unjust. Which confirm the justice and sovereignty of God who will ultimately judge all people according to their deeds.

Furthermore, Paul highlights a profound aspect of Christian living, maintaining a clear conscience before God and fellow humans. He expresses his commitment to living a life free from offense, actively striving to honor God and show kindness and fairness toward others. Paul's dedication to living with a clear conscience underscores the transformative power of God's words.

Protection and Intervention

Obedience to God's commands is depicted as the key to unlocking divine strength in times of trials, temptations and adversities. The promise that God will be "an enemy unto thine enemies, and an adversary unto thine adversaries" underscores the potent defensive and capabilities inherent in aligning one's actions with God's Word. This assurance serves as a source of comfort and empowerment when facing opposition or persecution. Words of God continue reaffirming trust in God's faithfulness and sovereignty.

Spiritual Empowerment

Obeying God's Word leads to transformative process to overcome obstacles and to fulfill God's purpose. By submitting to God's will and aligning actions with His commands, there comes ability to tap into a reservoir of divine grace and strength with confidence to navigate life's challenges. Godly empowerment transcends mere human effort to experience victories that defy natural limitations.

Trustworthiness Of God's Word

In Ezekiel 12:25-26, shows powerful inherent in God's word. The passage highlights the unwavering authority and reliability of God's word "For I am the LORD: I will speak, and the word that I shall speak shall come to pass; it shall be no more prolonged: for in your days, O rebellious house, will I say the word, and will not perform it, saith the Lord GOD." This verse reveals divine potency within God's word. It serves as a reminder that God's word is not subject to alteration by anyone. There is no partiality in God. Word of the LORD is correct. The fulfillment is certain and absolute. This assurance is not contingent upon human compliance or circumstance but stands firm in the sovereignty of God Himself. At times it may require actions and sometimes no action needed. It depends on supreme God by Him Self.

Ezekiel 12 illuminates the pivotal role of prophets as conduits for transmitting God's messages. It emphasizes the prophet's duty to faithfully convey divine words entrusted to them, irrespective of the audience's receptivity or the prevailing cultural climate. This passage serves as a beacon of hope and assurance. The message in Ezekiel 12 as illustrated in the previous pages stands as trustworthiness of God's promises and underscores the importance of taken God as His words. By embracing God's word with open hearts and minds, God's people can navigate life's challenges with confidence.

Reflecting on my own journey, I've witnessed the transformative power of God's word in my life.

Through moments of reflection and divine revelation, I've experienced the profound impact of aligning my life with the truth words of God which is shaping my character daily and propelling me towards a deeper authenticity in my faith journey. The acknowledgment of God's creative command and the transformative power of His word serves as a profound reminder of the importance of aligning one's own words and actions with God's words. Oracle of the LORD is written to harness the power of God's words.

Ezekiel 12:25-26 stands as a testament to the power and trustworthiness of God's word. It serves as a rallying cry for readers to anchor their lives upon the unshakeable foundation of divine truth, trusting in the fulfillment of God's promises and faithfully proclaiming His word to a world in need of hope and redemption. Words of God conveys the essence of God's odyssey as depicted in the Scriptures.

"God made a decree which shall not pass away" resonates as a testament to the eternal and unchanging nature of God's will. This statement is an anchor to steadfastness of God's words and assurance in the enduring principles established by God, the Creator of Heaven and Earth.

God commanded and were created" a statement that testify that the word of God is divine creativity. God's word has the capacity to speak life into existence. James 1:18 "He chose to give us birth through the word of truth, that we will be first fruits of all he created". "God commanded and were created" shows the boundless creativity through God's word. This statement underscores the enormous authority and power of God's word. God's word can effortlessly bring the world and all its wonders into existence. Just as God's words brought life and order to the world, humanities are reminded of their own capacity to speak life into existence. Words that are aligned with principles of goodness, truth, and divine will of God can foster creation, transformation, and positive change in the world.

James 1:18 reinforces the concept by emphasizing the transformative power of God's word in the lives of believers. "He chose to give us birth through the word of truth, that we might be a kind of first fruits of all he created." This verse highlights that human-beings are not just passive recipients but active participants in God's creative work. Through the word of truth, they experience spiritual rebirth, and become the "first fruits," or the initial and exemplary products of God's creation. This new birth signifies calling to live out the values of truth and goodness. Thereby reflecting the divine nature and contributing to the ongoing process of creation and renewal through God's word.

In the epistle of James, particularly in James 3:1 and 3:5, the power and responsibility of words are highlighted. James 3:1 warns, "Not many of you should become teachers, my fellow believers, because you know that we who teach will be judged more strictly." This verse underscores the weight of responsibility that comes with the use of words, especially in teaching and guiding others. James 3:5 further

ORACLE OF THE LORD

elaborates, "Likewise, the tongue is a small part of the body, but it makes great boasts. Consider what a great forest is set on fire by a small spark." Here, James emphasizes the immense power contained in words. Words are capable of creating significant impact, whether positive or negative.

Given this profound power in the Word of God, readers are encouraged to ensure their words serve as a source of encouragement and upliftment to those who hear them. Recognizing that God is in control of everyone and can instill a deep sense of peace and confidence to His children. This assurance eliminates the need to belittle others or to boast about self-achievements. Children of God identity and worth are secure in God's love and sovereignty. Recognizing the LORD is in control liberate intend compulsion to seek validation through harmful speech or self-aggrandizement.

Words should reflect the values of the Kingdom of God, values of love, grace, and encouragement. Words of encourages speaking with the intent to build , inspire, and to bring comfort to those around us. By doing so, is honoring God, reinforcing unity and edification of the community.

In practical terms, this means be mindful of words when interacting with other. Whether in personal conversations, public speaking, or online communication. They should strive to choose words that convey kindness, truth, and support. This mindful approach to speech is a powerful testament to personal faith and commitment to living according to guardians in God's word. The potent words of God, as emphasized in the book of James is a call to a higher standard of communication. Hence is important to let go of negative speech and embrace the call to encourage and uplift others. Which will then strengthen relationship and fosters positive outcome and nurtures good environment.

Unity

The word of God serves as a unifying force for many religious communities. It provides a common source of belief and practice fostering a sense of community among believers. It's important to note that the power of the word of God can vary among different religious denominations. However, for many, the word of God in the Bible is a profound and transformative force that guides, sustains, and shapes lives.

In Matthew 7:24-29, Jesus presents a powerful illustration of the significance of hearing and obeying His teachings. He likens those who hear His words and put them into practice to a wise person who builds their house upon a rock-solid foundation. When the storms of life inevitably come as it symbolized by rain, floods, and winds, still the wise person's house stands firm because of its secured footing on the rock. This description signifies the importance of anchoring one's life upon the unshakable truth and wisdom found in Jesus Christ. Those who heed His teachings and incorporate them into their lives establish a firm foundation that can withstand the trials and tribulations of life.

Jesus warns of the consequences for those who hear His words but fail to act upon them. He compares them to a foolish person who builds their house upon the shifting sand. When the storms rage, their house collapses because it lacks a stable foundation. Oracle of the LORD emphasizes the vital connection between hearing and doing. It's not enough to merely listen to words of God; true wisdom comes from putting God's words into action. Hence, true faith in God's word is demonstrates not only by professing but also by living out the principles and obedient to God's commandment.

Oracle of the LORD highlights God's promises to answer prayers. And encourage readers to allow God's words to dwell richly within them. This assurance reinforces the intimate relationship between humanity and God underscoring the significance of remaining steadfast in faith and obedience.

Ultimately, this book serves as a call to discipleship, urging them to build lives upon the solid foundation of Christ and to demonstrate faith through obedient to God's word. It a reminder that allegiance is to Christ, who purchased humanity with His blood and ultimate authority which lies in God's command. Trusting God's word is building live upon a solid foundation that cannot be shaken. Trust and faithfully follow God's command has great reward.

Chapter 20: The Oracle of God

Distinguished God's Word

God's Words reveal transformative power of God and the ability to touch hearts and inspire minds. Across cultures and continents, humanity has sought solace and wisdom through the bible. God's word offers a roadmap for righteous living, a blueprint for harmony and vision for higher purposes. Yet, the interpretation of God's Word is often fraught with complexities and controversies. In the midst of a world marked by strife and division, the relevance of "Distinguished God's Word" endures throughout history. Differences in understanding and application of God's words have led to schisms, conflicts, and violence. And yet, amidst the diverging voices, there remains a common thread, call to compassion, justice, and love. God's Word requires humility, openness, and willingness to wrestle with profound questions of existence and morality.

Nature and Creation

God's words are the beauty of the world. If words of God are misinterpreted it can bring complexity to the world. The world is the wonders of God's creation which confirms God's Divine intelligence. Nature stands as a testament to the divine power of God and God's infinite intelligence. Oracle of the LORD is an inspirational to study the word of God. God's word as a facilitator for the formation of the world and all that inhabits it. It shows the simplicity of God's words and yet profound effectiveness of God's words in bringing the complexities of life and entire word.

At the heart of the concept of nature and creation lies the recognition that the world with all its phenomena is not a product of chance or randomness but a deliberate expression of divine will and wisdom of Almighty God. There are various beliefs that nature manifests God's presence and reflects God's attributes.

The beauty and complexity of nature is the revelation of God's majesty and creative power. Each sunrise from the sky, bright moon, shining stars at night, breeze that whispers through the leaves, and each thunderstorm that unleashes its fury upon the earth bear witness to the awe-inspiring magnificence of God's power. For many, the contemplation of nature's wonders evokes sense of reverence and gratitude towards God the Creator. It inspires awe and humility in the face of the vastness and complexity of the world.

Nature serves as a source of nourishment and renewal. Whether through solitary walks in the wilderness, moments of quiet reflection, or the contemplation of a star-filled sky, people often find solace, inspiration, and sense of connection to something greater than themselves in the embrace of nature. God expects every human to cultivate deeper appreciation for the wonders of God creation and to steward it with care and reverence, recognizing it as a precious gift entrusted to mankind.

Creator and Creation

The Bible opens with "In the beginning, God created the heavens and the earth" (Genesis 1:1). God's spoken word brought the entire world into existence, demonstrating the creative and authoritative power in God word.

1. **Revelation:** The Bible is the inspired and authoritative word of God. It reveals God's character, will, and plan for humanity. Believers turn to the Bible for guidance, knowledge, and understanding of their faith.

2. **Transformation:** The word of God is a double-edged sword (Hebrews 4:12). It has the power to penetrate the depths of human heart, discerning thoughts and intentions. It can convict, challenge, and change lives leading to growth and transformation.

3. **Salvation:** The Bible conveys the message of salvation through faith in Jesus Christ. Many Christians believe that faith comes by hearing the word of God (Romans 10:17). Through God's word, people learn about God's love, grace, and the path to eternal life.

4. **Guidance:** The Bible provides moral and ethical guidance for believers, helping believers navigate life's challenges and making choices that align with God's will.

5.   **Comfort and Encouragement:** In times of hardship, people often turn to the Bible for comfort and encouragement. The promises and teachings found in Scripture offer solace and hope.

6.   **Authority:** The word of God is the ultimate authority in matters of faith and practice for many Christians. It shapes people beliefs, values, and the way they live their lives.

7.   **Prayer and Worship:** Many prayers and forms of worship are based on the words and teachings of the Bible. Believers find power and connection with God through the scriptures.

8.   **Unity:** The Bible serves as a unifying force for many religious communities. It provides a common source of belief and practice, fostering a sense of community among believers.

9.   **Endurance and Perseverance:** The stories and teachings in the Bible often highlight the importance of faith, endurance, and perseverance in the face of challenges and adversity. The word of God inspires journey of faith.

Inspiration and Intuition

Many believers believe moments of sudden inspiration or deep intuition to God's guidance. God sometimes communicates with individual on a personal level through inner prompting.

Miracles and Supernatural

Miracles and supernatural occurrences happen to people as signs of God's intervention. Miracles range from healing to extraordinary coincidences. Miracles and supernatural events often capture human belief in God awesome words across cultures and religions. Occurrences of miracles are seen as divine interventions or words from God. Miracles and supernatural events are vast and encompasses everything from healing to extraordinary transpires that defy rational explanation.

Healing miracles are among the most well-known phenomena, mostly instances where individuals experience sudden and inexplicable recoveries from illness or injury. These occurrences are attributed to God intervention, prayers, or the intercession of saints. Stories of terminally ill patients making miraculous recoveries or individuals being cured of chronic conditions have been reported throughout history and continue to inspire awe and faith.

Beyond physical healing, miracles and supernatural events can also manifest in emotional healing. People may experience profound shifts in consciousness, finding inner peace, clarity, or a sense of purpose following supernatural encounter or divine intervention through God's word. Extraordinary coincidences or miracles are category of miracles and supernatural events. These are instances where seemingly unrelated events align in a way that defies statistical probability or logical explanation. Examples include chance encounters that lead to life-changing opportunities, timely interventions that avert disaster, or the sudden appearance of resources exactly when needed most. While skeptics may dismiss such occurrences as mere chance, believers often interpret them as signs of God guidance or providence at work.

It's important to note that interpretations of miracles and supernatural events vary widely across different belief systems and cultural contexts. What is considered a miracle in one tradition might be viewed skeptically or explained differently in another. Nevertheless, the enduring fascination phenomena speaks to humanity's enduring quest for meaning, connection, and transcendent in the words of God. Whether as signs of divine presence, is a reminder of the truths or simply moments of wonder and awe. Miracles and supernatural events continue to inspire faith, hope, and curiosity in people around the world.

Consistency and Discernment

Messages that align with the scripture and God's revelation are divine. Consistency with established God's word is a key factor in discernment. This involves understanding God's word, seeking guidance through prayer, meditation, and consultation through God's word and messages. Personal experiences of a deep sense of peace, clarity, or profound transformation can serve as confirmation of the divine God's word.

Fruits of the Spirit

The "fruits of the Spirit" (love, joy, peace, patience, kindness, goodness, faithfulness, gentleness, and self-control) are benchmark for discernment. The ways God communicates His words are diverse and personal. Discerning messages from Almighty God involves the combination of guidance, personal experiences and commitment to loving God's principles.

Love and Unfailing Promises

In the profound affirmation that "God loves humanity and cares for His promises shows the depths of divine affection and the unwavering commitment of God towards His creation. God's love to mankind extends beyond measure. God promises always stands, if truly is God promised. God's promises stand as a testament to God's integrity and His caring character. God's love is remarkable that God's love for humanity is intricately woven into the fabric of His promises.

The very act of God caring for His promises is an expression of His deep affection and concern for the well-being of humanity, He created. It underscores the idea that divine love is not merely a sentiment but a driving force behind the fulfillment of God's command. God's love and promises affirms God as a faithful and caring Creator. It highlights the reliability of His word, grounded in love that surpasses human comprehension. It serves as assurance, knowing God is in control and God's love never falters. Is important to reflect on the transformative impact of incorporating God's Word into daily life, recognizing that it emanates from heart flowing with love and concern.

"God's love for humanity and cares for His promises" serves as a profound reminder of the inseparable connection between divine love and the fulfillment of God's commitments. Oracle of the LORD invites believers to anchor their faith in the enduring God's love, finding assurance and strength in the magnificence of His Word.

God's Commands

"God commanded and were created," ls a timeless truth across the span of existence. This statement captures the awe-inspiring creative power inherent in God's commandments. God's commands are not mere words, but potent forces that bring forth God existence. The very act of God commands sets into motion the miraculous process of creation, a testament to the unmatched authority and creative proficiency of the Almighty God.

God's commands result in creation emphasizes the intentional and purposeful nature of God Almighty. It is a divine plan and design wherein every element and entity find its origin in the word of God. The scripture often calls to reflect on the authority and sovereignty of God's word. God's commands have the power to summon existence to a level of control and mastery over all that is created. It fosters a sense of trust and reliance on God divine will, acknowledging that every aspect of creation is intricately linked to Words of God.

God commanded and creation unfolds deep reverence for God's word. It encourages a mindfulness of the power embedded in our own words and the potential impact they can have on the world around us. "God commanded and were created" shows the creativity, acknowledgement and the authority of God's word. This worthy of emulation to speak life into existence through words that align with the principles of goodness and truth.

This impact of God's word on Paul's life and mission shows the transformative power of Scripture which not only informs but also shapes character and conduct. People can find hope and strength in the assurance of resurrection through faith in God's word and obedience to God's word. Is important to have clear conscience. Clear conscience to honor God and show kindness to others. The efficacy of God's word is seen not only in doctrinal beliefs but also in moral conduct and ethical behavior. It is an inspiration to walk in integrity and righteousness, guided by deep reverence to God's commands.

Chapter 21: Application of God's Word

Alignment with Love and Compassion

Writing this book has been a journey of inspiration and discovery for me. My hope is that it inspires readers to explore deeply into God's Word and bring glory to God Almighty. The true messages of God are rooted in love, compassion, and a profound concern for the well-being of humanity. Messages that promote peace, justice, and kindness originate from God the Father, the Son, and the Holy Spirit.

The power of God's Word is a central theme of Oracle of the LORD. God's Word is a source of divine guidance, wisdom, and transformative influence. Psalm 105 reminds us that when the time is right, He sends His Word to fulfill His purposes. Numerous chapters and verses in Oracle of the LORD, this book illustrates the power of God's Word. "In the beginning, God created the heavens and the earth" (Genesis 1:1). God's spoken word brought the entire world into existence, demonstrating the creative and authoritative power of His Word. The words of God reveal God's character, will, and plan for humanity.

The Tapestry of Virtue

Exploring the characteristics transformed through God's word reveals how personal values and societal influences are interconnected. "The Tapestry of Virtue" examines common moral behaviors prevalent in today's world, such as choice, integrity, mercy, peace, love, and the impact of social media. This exploration consists intricacies of virtues, while also analyzing the profound effects of social media. Through thoughtful reflection, dialogue, and action, people can cultivate good virtues and contribute to a compassionate and harmonious world. The following series of applications of the Tapestry of Value are extracted from my previous blogs posted in www.perfectloveffl.com. "The Tapestry of Virtue" is a blog and invitation to embark on a journey of self-discovery and societal reflection, weaving together the threads of actions, experiences, and aspirations.

Taste or tasteless

Jesus called his followers the salt of the earth. What does this mean? God is looking for flavor or good characteristic from His people. Not many people like to eat tasteless food. Many will prefer to eat tasteful food. God requires people to produce good fruits.

What kind of fruits do you produce? Thought of evil is rotten or bitter fruit productions. Thoughts of evil and every thought of wickedness is not tasteful but bitter. Life is not a rehearsal as in preparation for upcoming show. Life is purposeful. As a salt in the world, everyone needs to purposely add tasteful seasons or flavors to daily encounters and activities.

Jesus was very straight forward. He told his people simply to: "Love the Lord your God with all your heart, soul, mind, and strength. And love your neighbors as yourself". As a salt of the earth Jesus expects his children to have a nature that is inwardly and outwardly loving. He doesn't want people to disguise ruthless nature in deception and selfishness. Christ employs His followers to give water to the weary to drink and bread to the hungry to eat. A good steward does not waste excess of common necessity. Any opportunity should be used to add value not to exploit and affiliate pains on others, especially the helpless. The arms of fatherless or helpless should not be broken.

The summary of this passage is using every opportunity as enhancement. The passage is an inspiration to be part of a solution at all times, places, workplaces, Communities, Schools, or anywhere or circumstances. Addition to purpose should be a desire to add value or enhancement in every situation instead of being an obstacle or a spoiler.

The scripture encourages believers to do unto others whatever they would love others to do unto them. "So, in everything, do to others what you would have them do to you, for this sums up the Law and the Prophets." (Matthew 7:12) "Love the Lord your God with all your heart and with all your soul and with all your mind and with all your strength. The second is this: 'Love your neighbor as yourself. There is no commandment greater than these." (Mark 12:30-31(NIV).

Choice or Taste is regarded as refinement of discernment. It encompasses choices and values. In a world inundated with options and distractions, cultivating a discerning taste becomes paramount guidance towards what is noble, uplifting, and true.

Integrity

Integrity stands as the cornerstone of character, reflecting the alignment between one's beliefs, words, and actions. It is the steadfast commitment to honesty, transparency, and moral uprightness, even in the face of adversity or temptation. In a society where ethical standards are sometimes compromised for personal gain, integrity serves as a beacon of light, illuminating the path of righteousness and honor.

Mercy

Mercy is an expression of compassion and forgiveness. Mercy holds the power to heal wounds, mend relationships, and foster reconciliation. It transcends judgment and retribution, offering grace and understanding to those who have erred or suffered. In a world marked by conflict and strife, the practice of mercy becomes a transformative force, bridging unity and fostering empathy and understanding.

Peace

Peace, the elusive pursuit of harmony and tranquility is both an inner state of being and a collective aspiration. It arises from the resolution of conflict, the cultivation of empathy, and the recognition of shared humanity. In an age of discord and unrest, nurturing peace requires courage, empathy, and a commitment to dialogue and understanding.

Love

Love is one of the most profound and universal virtues. It encompasses compassion, empathy, and selflessness, transcending the boundaries of race, religion, and nationality, and uniting us in a common bond of humanity. In a world yearning for connection and belonging, the practice of love becomes a transformative force, enriching lives and inspiring acts of kindness and generosity. Only God can truly bestow mercy, peace, and love upon anyone. God sent His Son, Jesus Christ, to redeem, adopt, and preserve His people, claiming ownership of His children.

As a result, everyone has the right and access to God's love and goodness. The love of God through Christ establishes a relationship with God as that of a father and child (Galatians 4:4-5 KJV). We worship God for His faithfulness, trustworthiness, care, generosity, kindness toward us and for God's sake. Though our love for God is a token of our devotion, it can never fully compare to who God is to humanity. God created the heavens, the earth, and everything in the world. What could be greater than that? Worshiping God is an acknowledgment of who God is, His mercy, love, and all the blessings He alone provides to humanity without prejudice. God is gracious and gentle to all. As Job 10:12 (KJV) says, "Thou hast granted me life and favor, and thy visitation hath preserved my spirit."

Impact of Social media

Social media platforms are great avenues of blessings if utilized in truth. Through social media platforms many people are able to connect with relations and desired audiences. Marketers are able to build brands with great contents. However, lots of lies are communicated daily through social media because some people are seeking approval of others without validation.

The impacts of integrity and virtues are gradually losing strength to social ills. Morality is diminishing, aspiration for fame and riches are rising in this era. People are scorning the truth and complacent about the truth of God. While many are leaning towards immorality and some zealous towards social peril. Vanity and fake grandeurs are receiving louder applause and there are high levels of competition for attention; even among strangers who do not really care or offer things of value.

What can be done to utilize the best social media offers to the world? Calling lovers of truth and those with the ability to understand to share uplifting messages. False statements and actions need to be shown. Reality must be embraced. There is a need for urgency to search and embrace truthfulness now. Consider the well-being of next Generations. There is a need for the next Generations to know what is true, admirable, and reality.

Amidst this exploration of virtue, the impact of social media looms large, shaping people's perceptions, influencing behaviors, and reshaping the fabric of society. While social media platforms offer unprecedented opportunities for connection, expression, and activism, they also pose challenges to people well-being, privacy, and the fabric of social discourse. Understanding interplay between social media and virtue is essential for navigating the complexities of digital age with wisdom, discernment, and integrity.

Legal Vs Ethics

Legal or Law refers to man-made system of rules. Legal is a system established by Authority, such as the Government, Organizations or the Societies to determine rights or wrongs, justices and fairness. Legal actions are normally decided by the courts. Ethics are moral principles that govern people's behaviors. Ethical behaviors are considered as acts of fairness, honesty, equity, and integrity. Sometimes, some decision makers face ethical dilemmas and legal consequences when making decisions. People have the ability to observe, identify, instruct, confront and punish. Only God can ascertain right from wrong because God weighs the hearts and intents.

The word of God is superb, impartial, same forever and needs no validation and approval. God is the only righteous Judge that has all authority on earth to correct and reprove. Words of God take prominence over Legal and Ethics if applied correctly. Basic ethics include morals and values based on histories, traditions or knowledge of rights or wrongs. Moral behaviors are conducts learned and accepted by people as standard of principle of right and wrong. Values or beliefs are acts the Societies or Organizations consider desirable. Sometimes non-ethical considerations have strong desires and can make decision makers choose non ethical actions above ethical actions. Another concern regarding ethical principles is that it is possible to value one ethical principle more than others.

The importance of ethical value is to balance good consequences above evil for the overall well-being of everyone. Hence, Ethical and Legal decisions are both complex. Legal consider consequential factors such as harm or benefit to the society or each concerned party. Legal decisions are persuasive authorities and subject to changes. Sometimes, legal and ethical decisions conflict with each other. Decision makers seeking for Justice and fairness are then left with the option to evaluate consequence and beneficial outcomes.

Decision makers calculate and analyze impact of decisions based on historical consequences and their knowledge. Legal and Ethics are subject to changes. Justice and judgement can be influenced by powerful defense or by high price. Sometimes legal or ethical interpretation may be partial or considered unreasonable. But the Word of God remains fair and truthful. Oracle of the LORD is "As it Is" forever. The words of the LORD are pure words as silver tried in a furnace of earth purified seven times according to Psalm 12 verse 6. "The Lord gave the word: great was the company of those that published it." Psalm 68:11 KJV.

New Creature

God gave a commandment to love one another as He loves Humanities. Which means love must be the center of whatever you do. If love is not the center of whatever you do, everything may be nothing. The Word of God is a command to be obeyed. Obeying God's commands strengthens the grace of God, brings comforts and resolutions. "This is my commandment, that ye love one another, as I have loved you" (John 15:12 KJV)

There is no need to trouble others, compare yourself with others' achievements or envy people because they seem to have achieved more than you. Why should you envy anyone? Blessings of God are not always outward things that can be seen or measured neither rites nor ceremonies to be noticed. Riches and happiness come from within, not the outward appearance. Sometimes those things that are outward may be temporary and sometimes may be faked or packaged.

Hence the bible says anyone who envies others is not wise because he or she cannot see far or has knowledge of the unseen aspects. God's blessings can manifest in righteousness, peace, and joy in the Holy Ghost. Christians are the temple of God. As the Temple which God dwells in, love, humility, and meekness are the greatest manifestation of Christ through His children. Christ in the heart of a man, is more than material blessings. Your nature testifies that God lives in you and works through you. If it is true that God works through you, every credit or discredit belongs to God.

"For we are God's fellow workers [His servants working together]; you are God's cultivated field [His garden, His vineyard], God's building" (1 Corinthians

3:9AMP). "And his "workmanship, created in Christ Jesus unto good works" (Ephesians 2:10). "Therefore, if any man be in Christ, he is a new creature: old things are passed away; behold, all things are become new." (2 Corinthians 5:17 KJV).

Expressions of "Unfeigned love"

Unfeigned love is pure love that occurs between people without romantic attraction. The type of LOVE discussed through this book is Unfeigned love or Agape love. 2nd Corinthians 6:6 says, "By pureness, by knowledge, by Long suffering, by kindness, by the Holy Ghost, by Love unfeigned" (KJV).

As I read this verse, "**Unfeigned love**" attracted my attention and amplified loudly in my heart. Unfeigned love means loving others without hypocrisy, acting, pretending, or with an aim for a selfish interest. 1 John 4:21 KJV explains the truth about unfeigned love; "he who loveth God loves his brother also." Which means to love God you must love your brothers, sisters, neighbors, people connected or related to you in any form. Love Unfeigned is most needed in a time like this. Unfeigned love characteristics can only be developed through the love of Jesus Christ.

Most love actions are feigned love. Feigned love is a counterfeit or hypocritical love, which is fake love or insincere love. True love is a manifestation of genuine, authentic love towards a person or people. The Bible says to love God is more than to know him. God wants people to genuinely love others as themselves. Though some people may be difficult to love, such difficulties can be overcome by recognizing there is no perfect person on earth. Everyone of us has a trait or traits of imperfection.

Manifestation of unfeigned love reveals the level of love a person has for God. Whether a person is a true or hypocritical Christian, "By their fruit you shall know them." LOVE is what determines love for God and faith in Jesus Christ. According to 1 John 4:20. "If a man says, I love God, and hates his brother, he is a liar: for he that loveth not his brother whom he hath seen, how can he love God whom he hath not seen?"

Therefore, anyone that hates someone created in God's image does not know the true God." Everyone that loveth is born of God, and knoweth God. He that loveth not knoweth not God." (1 John 4:7,8) (KJV) History has revealed that lack of love is the major source of problems all over the Globe. Problems starting from friends, families, relations, communities, workplaces, schools etc. are as a result of lack of unfeigned love. Most of the problems in the world can be eschewed or resolved if authentic or unfeigned love exists among people of all categories, tribes, nations, and all circles of sphere. Loving and knowing God is one and cannot be separated from each other.

Think about this for a moment; knowing God without a pure love for people is vain and pointless. How can God be pleased; If people hate others, instigate or initiate pains, spoils, harms or hinder someone made in God's Image? Characteristics of a true God is sincere and real love. God's children must manifest their Godly character. The Bible says" "He who lacks pure love for a friend, family or brethren is blind, and cannot see afar off, and hath forgotten that he was purged from his old sins."

For example, people who manifest unfeigned love or agape Love or willful or pure love will always be happy when a friend or family member or others are happy. While people without unfeigned love may feel sad because of another person's achievement. A person without unfeigned love may be happy to hear negative reports about others. Such people delight to hear about other people's wrongdoing rather than what they did right. That kind of feeling is feigned love not unfeigned love. A person that has Agape love or Spirit of Christ will rather pray on behalf of others and urge to help instead of rejoicing for their misfortune. Evidence of unfeigned, pure, or undefiled love is to feel for others as you would feel for yourself in such a situation.

Knowing and accepting Jesus as LORD and SAVIOR is by Faith: Exercising sincere love for others can be by faith too. It does not mean a person should force his or her love on others or keep on accepting hate in return for love. One of the lessons thought by Jesus Christ is "dust off your feet" "And whosoever shall not receive you, nor hear your words, when ye depart out of that house or city, shake off the dust of your feet." (Matthew 10:14 KJV).

Love those who welcomed your love and keep off from those using your loving nature as a weakness against you. May the LORD grant all a compassionate heart and spirit of empathy toward others In Jesus Name.

Moral Imperative

Obedience to God's Word is a moral imperative that reflects a deeper commitment to knowing God. To "obey his voice and do all that He speak" underscores the importance of aligning one's actions with God's moral standards and ethical principles. This call to obedience is rooted in the recognition of God's authority and sovereignty over every aspect of human existence. The scripture emphasizes the important to live lives characterized by integrity, humility, and compassion.

The verse from Exodus 23:22 serves as an important reminder of the transformative power and inherent authority of God's Word. Through obedience to God's commands, people can experience divine protection, intervention, and empowerment. Thereby fulfilling God-given destinies and bearing witness to His faithfulness and sovereignty. People become living testimonies as they continue to align their lives with His will. Words of God can shape lives and course of history.

In absence of God, finding true refuge becomes an elusive pursuit. Without acknowledgement of God, there is dénouement of the foundational source of strength, wisdom, and guidance that anchors the life. God serves as the cornerstone of existence, providing stability and direction in times of uncertainty. Without His presence, many people will be drifted and become vulnerable to the noises in the world.

Apart from God, there exists no sustenance for soul, no fountain of wisdom to draw from, and no helper to turn to in moments of need. Every aspect of human being finds its fulfillment and purpose in relationship with God. God is the ultimate refuge, the unwavering anchor that steadies the course amidst life's storms.

Attempting to navigate life without God is akin to sailing a ship without a compass or chart. It leads to aimless wandering and eventual shipwreck. In contrast, with God as a refuge, believers find sanctuary in His unconditional love, unwavering presence, and boundless grace. Of God.

Ultimately, without God, life lacks meaning, purpose, and direction. God is not merely a supplemental source of strength or guidance but the very essence of existence. Therefore, in the absence of God, there is emptiness and despair.

Righteousness through Christ

"For they being ignorant of God's righteousness," This part refers to some people who, according to Paul, lack understanding or knowledge about the righteousness that comes from God. Righteousness in this context, means being morally right or just in the eyes of God. "Than people trying to establish their own righteousness," This part says instead of relying on God's righteousness, some people establish their own righteousness, trying to attain moral or spiritual perfection on their own, through adherence to laws and rituals, rather than through faith in God.

"Have not submitted themselves unto the righteousness through Christ" This part indicates that because some people rely on their own efforts rather than God's righteousness, they had not submitted themselves to God's way of righteousness. The scripture criticizes people for relying on their own works and rituals to attain righteousness instead of accepting the righteousness that comes from God through faith. God's word highlights the importance of faith in God's righteousness rather than relying on human efforts alone.

Guidance Against Fear and Conspiracy

Isaiah recounts how the Lord communicated to him with strength and clarity, instructing him not to follow the ways of the people around him. The Lord tells Isaiah not to adopt the mindset of fear and conspiracy that is prevalent among the people. Specifically, Isaiah 8:11-12 (KJV), "for the Lord spoke thus to me with a strong hand and instructed me that I should not walk in the way of this people, saying." That he should not walk in the way of this people emphasizes the importance of maintaining a different path, one guided by God's wisdom rather than the fears and suspicions of human society.

Furthermore, Isaiah was instructed not to be afraid of the threats made by the people nor to be troubled by their fears. This highlights the importance of trusting in God's protection and sovereignty rather than succumbing to the anxieties and intimidations of the world. Overall, this passage serves as a reminder of the importance of staying grounded in faith and not being swayed by prevailing fears or conspiracy theories. It encourages reliance on God's guidance and protection, even in the face of uncertainty and opposition.

Faith in God's Word

The gospel of Jesus Christ teaches that salvation comes through grace. True faith in God, naturally leads to good works. Faith is inherently actionable and serves as the driving force that energizes the word of God. While people may show favoritism, God's word applies to everyone equally. Therefore, faith must always be aligned with God's word.

Accurate Word of God

Believers sometimes ponder the role of prophets throughout history; men and women called to deliver messages from God to His people. While some may question the accuracy of every pronouncement made by prophets, but it cannot be dismissed by the undeniable instances of prophetic insight and foresight that have shaped the course of human history. Is also important to acknowledge the fallibility of humanity, understanding that even the most devout prophets may grapple with their own limitations and interpretations.

Oracle of the LORD offer a testament to the accuracy and power of God's word not solely based on theological assertions or doctrinal arguments, but rather on personal experience. I have witnessed the transformative impact of God's word in my own life and the lives of those around me. let us embrace the mystery and wonder of God's word with humility, let us approach the scriptures with reverence and discernment, seeking wisdom and illumination from the Holy Spirit. Let us honor the prophetic tradition while acknowledging the human frailty inherent in its delivery. May readers quest for truth and understanding lead them closer to the heart of God, where accuracy and power of God are revealed in fullness.

"But ye are a chosen generation, a royal priesthood, a holy nation, a peculiar people; that ye should shew forth the praises of him who hath called you out of darkness into his marvelous light" (1 peter 2:9 KJV) Hebrews 1:1-2 KJV "God, who at sundry times and in divers' manners spake in time past unto the fathers by the prophets hath in these last days spoken unto us by his Son, whom he hath appointed heir of all things, by whom also he made the worlds" Revelation 21.3 ESV. "And I heard a loud voice from the throne saying, "Behold, the dwelling place of God is with man. He will dwell with them and they will be his people, and God".

Obedience to God's Word

Obedience and faith are inseparably linked, each reinforcing the other. Faith is never solitary; it manifests through obedient and actions. As Jesus said, "Let your light shine before others." This means living out God's word in a way that visibly demonstrates His love and truth to the world. Obedience to God's word involves aligning our actions with His will, reflecting our faith through a life that honors God.

Reflection on Being a Living Oracle

A living Oracle carries the presence of God, with His Spirit dwelling within, empowering them to fulfill the divine mandate and impact the world for God's sake. As vessels of His grace, expressions of His glory, channels of His mercy, and bearers of His light, living Oracles embody God's purpose. To be a living Oracle of the LORD is to walk in alignment with His will, fully surrendering to His divine plan.

Reflecting on this profound truth reveals my purpose in the journey of fulfilling God's calling. As a living Oracle of the LORD, I am not a product of chance or circumstance but intentionally created and fashioned by God Himself. In His wisdom and sovereignty, He has imbued me with a unique purpose, positioning me as a conduit of His love and a reflection of His glory.

We are not created to merely exist in the mundane and ordinary, but to transcend. Each person is set apart for a divine purpose. Every breath we take, and every step we tread is infused with the presence and power of God. Our lives are called to radiate His love and reflect His glory to the world around us. Being a living Oracle means surrendering personal agendas and desires to God's will, trusting that He who began a good work will bring it to completion.

As an Oracle of the LORD, I recognize the profound privilege and responsibility entrusted to me by God Almighty. "I have written unto you according to God's Word" resonates both as a declaration and an invitation. It is a declaration of faith, testifying to God's goodness as the steward of this message. It is also an acknowledgment that every word in this book reflects the eternal truths found in the Holy Scriptures and the words from Almighty God. Truly, "God is not slack concerning His promises." His words are an unshakable foundation and a steadfast anchor, promises fulfilled yesterday, today, and forevermore. He who promised is faithful to fulfill. As John 6:63 (KJV) reminds us, "It is the spirit that quickeneth; the flesh profiteth nothing: the words that I speak unto you, they are spirit, and they are life."

I have written according to the ability given to me, trusting God to bring His word to fulfillment.

Salvation

Salvation is a central of Christianity. Salvation leads to deliverance from sin and eternal separation from God. Salvation is only attainable through Jesus Christ. Acts 4:12 in the Bible states, "Neither is there salvation in any other: for there is none other name under heaven given among men whereby we must be saved." Christianity is the acknowledgment of sinfulness. As Romans 3:23 declares, "For all have sinned and come short of the glory of God." This acknowledgment is the first step towards salvation.

It's an acceptance of personal wrongdoing and a recognition of the need for divine forgiveness.

Christians demonstrate faith through prayer of salvation declaration. "I confess my sins and acknowledge Jesus as my LORD and Savior. Who died for my sins and rose from the dead. I ask the LORD Jesus Christ to forgive my sins, Come into my heart and life. Purify my soul and body, renew my heart and make me your child." This prayer signifies a surrender to Christ, inviting believers into life of transformation and redemption.

It's a declaration of trust in Jesus as the only means of salvation and a commitment to follow Him. Through this act of faith, humanities are reconciled with God, becoming recipients of His grace and mercy. The path to salvation begins with repentance and faith in Jesus Christ. One must acknowledge sins and ask for forgiveness, believing that Jesus is the Son of God who died for our sins and rose from the dead. Central to this understanding is the exclusivity of Christ as the mediator between humanity and God. Jesus Himself proclaimed, "I am the way and the truth and the life. No one comes to the father except through me" (John 14:6). This statement underscores the belief that salvation is found solely in Christ.

The promise of salvation extends beyond forgiveness of sins to restoration and reconciliation with God. Christ's faithfulness ensures that those who believe in Him are not only forgiven but also adopted as children of God. As stated in the prayer of salvation, believers are purified, renewed, and made heirs of God's promises.

Salvation through Jesus Christ is the cornerstone of Christian faith. It's a journey of repentance, faith, and surrender, concluding the reconciliation with God and the assurance of eternal life. Through Christ, believers find forgiveness, restoration, and a renewed relationship with

God. Isaiah 53:8 serves as a guiding light, inspiring those seeking the depths of salvation through Jesus Christ to embark on the journey of faith

"Oracle of the LORD" encourages readers not only to understand the words but to enter into the very essence of the meaning of the word of God. In light of these truths, embrace God's word and godliness. Let God's words be seasoned with grace, actions be guided by love, and lives become living testimony to the transformative power of God's Word. May readers of this book walk in righteousness, clothed in the armor of faith, and equipped with the sword of the Spirit of Almighty God, which is the Word of God.

Conclusion

Oracle of the LORD is not merely an intellectual pursuit but a transformative journey of the heart and soul. *The book* was not written from an abundance of knowledge on the topic, but out of obedience to God's calling. The words in *Oracle of the LORD* are drawn from Scripture, divine revelation, and the rhema word of God. The true power of God's Word is not found in the elegance of language or the age of the text, but in its ability to inspire human hearts toward goodness, kindness, and compassion. Its ultimate purpose is to transform and uplift lives, leaving an enduring legacy of God's Word.

God's Word is perfect and unchanging truth. It is accurate, consistent, and transformative. God's words have the power to shape lives, are living and active, and bring fulfillment to all who trust in it. Words that can never expired but remain relevant throughout history, today, and into the future. God's Word is everlasting and dependable, offering guidance and hope for every generation. *"For the word of God is living and active. Sharper than any double-edged sword, it penetrates even to dividing soul and spirit, joints and marrow; it judges the thoughts and attitudes of the heart."* (Hebrews 4:12) *"The grass withers and the flowers fall, but the word of our God endures forever."* (Isaiah 40:8) God's Word is eternal, powerful, and never failing.

Conclusion

Oracle of the LORD invites readers to partake in the priceless treasure God offers through His Word and through the atoning work of Christ. As you engage with these divine truths. Through revelation, scripture, guidance, and teaching, may you explore the profound significance inherent in God's Word. I hope the *Oracle of the LORD* will inspire at least someone to live a life aligned with God's will. May the reality truth in God's words transforms the readers' heart and mind to remain open, allowing the Word of God to ignite deeper intimacy with the Almighty God. In Jesus' name, Amen!

About the Author

Christie is a devoted wife, mother, and grandmother, as well as a successful small business owner in the United States. Despite not initially having the opportunity to attend high school, her faith and perseverance guided her to remarkable achievements. Through God's grace, she earned her high school diploma and went on to complete a Bachelor of Social Sciences (BSS) and an MBA. In addition to her accomplishments in business, Christie is a passionate author, having written several books that reflect her journey of resilience and faith.

Dedication

To God Almighty,

All glory be unto You, O LORD, for You are worthy of all praises and honors! As I dedicate this book, *"Oracle of the LORD,"* into Your hands, I am humbled by Your mighty works and your excellent greatness. You are the source of all inspiration, wisdom, resources, and strength. I acknowledge Your hand guiding me throughout the journey of writing this book. I offer my heartfelt thanks to You for granting me victory through Jesus Christ. It is through His grace and power that I have been able to bring this work to fruition. Every word on these pages is a testament to Your faithfulness and love.

May this book bring glory to Your Name and serve as a vessel for Your truth and grace to touch the lives of those who read it. May it inspire hearts, uplift spirits, and draw others closer to You. In Jesus name, I dedicate this book, *"Oracle of the LORD,"* to You, O God, with gratitude, Amen!